Right Relationships

How to create them and how to restore them

Tom Marshall

Sovereign World

Sovereign World Ltd
PO Box 784
Ellel
Lancaster LA1 9DA
England
www.sovereignworld.com

Bible quotations are taken from the King James Version, also from
the New International Version of the Holy Bible. Copyright © 1973,
1978 International Bible Society. Published by Hodder & Stoughton.

ISBN 978 1 85240 495 6

Front cover design by Andrew Mark, ThirteenFour Design
Typeset by CRB Associates, Reepham, Norfolk
Printed in Malta

Contents

Page

4

Contents

Foreword

Relationships can be both the greatest source of joy, and at the same time the greatest source of sorrow. Fortunately, in this book by Tom Marshall, we have a resource that avoids a shallow "glanceover" approach, but one that takes the reader to a deep level which can bring about new insights and understanding.

I especially appreciate a book which combines depth and practicality. This is such a book. The content discussed is essential for valued and long-lasting relationships. The style makes it easy to read, and also applicable to existing or future relationships. The chapter on trust and honor speaks to issues which seem to be either hidden or lost in many relationships. Hopefully the guidance provided by the author will go a long way in helping all of us build quality and God-honoring relationships.

H. Norman Wright

Introduction

This is a book about relationships. Not any particular type of relationship like marriage or employment or church life, but about relationships in general, what they are, how they work, how they can go wrong and more importantly, how they can be put back together again.

We need a book like this for several reasons. One is that unless we understand how relationships were designed by God to function in the first place, we are left with try-as-you-go or copy-a-model methods as our chief way of discovering how you do it. That is how most of us acquired what relational skills we possess, but even if they work fairly well there is a lot to be said for taking a little time out for more formal instruction. It is likely to improve our performance no end.

The second reason is even more important. Unless we know how relationships are meant to function and what it takes to keep them growing we can reach breaking point and not even know what has brought us to this crisis. A very common state of mind of people in the midst of a relationship break-up is sheer puzzlement. "How on earth did we get ourselves into a mess like this?" "We started out really loving one another, now it ends in this tangle. How?" Finally when we are in this state of uncertainty and confusion we are poorly placed to know what to do to get the relationship back on the rails again.

I have to confess however that the book was also written out of the struggle, even the agony of finding that Christians seem on the whole to have just as many relational problems as do unbelievers. Moreover, although we ought to be the experts in understanding and changing human nature our track record in repairing stressed relationships and restoring those that have broken down does not bear that out. Truth to tell, it is little better than the results achieved by secular counsellors, and neither record is much to get wildly enthusiastic about.

When however, I was driven back to basics to ask the fundamental questions I ought to have asked in the first place, and to ask them of the Designer's handbook, I began to see light at the end of the tunnel. Scripture, I discovered, not only addresses the nature of relationships and the factors that are necessary to make them work, it spells out the startling dynamic of restoration in a way that gave me more hope than I would have believed possible a few years ago. Experience has proved, to me at least, that this hope has not been ill founded. I live today in eager expectation that there is still more to understand and more to put into practice.

Chapter 1

Relationships – the Central Category

It would be difficult indeed to exaggerate the importance of the subject of relationships. I now realise that for a long time I treated them as somehow peripheral. They were on the circumference of my life where my life impacted on or interacted with other lives. Now I see that relationships are the most central factor of our very existence as human beings. We spend our lives in a veritable network of relationships and cut off from them we die. With very little difficulty the average person could tally a dozen to twenty different types of relationships in which they participate in the course of a single day. And yet we take very little time to consider the raw material of which these interactions consist.

Perhaps that is one reason why they cause us so much trouble, because the truth is that most of our problems stem from difficulties in relationships. Marital and family problems, vocational, business and societal problems, religious, racial and industrial strife, political and international tensions, all have to do with relationships that are not working. The thrust of all temptation and the primary effect of all sin is to disrupt relationships. The end result is what both the Bible and psychology call alienation – estrangement or separation from God, from others and from the world, and the inability to choose and act in relationships. The time is overdue for us to think seriously about the whole subject, beginning, I suggest with both an anatomy of relationships, and a pathology. Otherwise, with the best intentions in the world, we are like a doctor trying to mend a broken leg or diagnose a disease without ever having studied the anatomy or physiology of the human body.

An understanding of the subject of relationships is still more

9

important because it affects our experience of God. It was life-changing for me, years ago, to realise that we relate to God in exactly the same way as we relate to other people. In other words we use the same bits of us in both areas. There are many people who do not have a close relationship with God, or do not really understand how to have a relationship with God because they have difficulty relating at all or simply do not know how to do it. And for many others, sadly, the language of the church has so mystified the whole thing that knowing God appears to them to be some strange mystical experience that only a few religiously orientated people ever discover.

The truth is that relationships lie at the very core of the entire biblical revelation concerning God and man.

1. **The first statements made by God concerning man that he had created were, firstly**, *"Let us make man in our image."*[1] Man in other words was created to be a God-imager, that is, to model his life and character on that of God. But the God that man images is a God of eternal, infinite relationships – Father, Son and Spirit. **Secondly**, *"It is not good for the man to be alone."*[2] Henceforth man in the Bible is always man-in-relationships. We are vulnerable on our own, and our greatest dread and greatest anguish is always loneliness.

"Two are better than one, because they have a good return for their work: if one falls down, his friend can help him up. But pity the man who falls and has no one to help him up!"[3]

2. **In the Bible life and death are a matter of relationships**. To be in relationship with God, the Source of Life is to be alive; to be separated from God, the Source of Life is to be dead. I may walk around, laugh, eat, fight and sleep but I am dead. It all depends on my relationship with him.

That is why *righteousness* is at root a relational term. It means to be rightly related or in the old English term to be "rightwise" with one another. We can always tell in a moment when we are not rightwise with our spouse, or with our friend. Even a term like the *fear of the Lord* turns out to express not awe or numinous dread but a quality of relationship. To the ancient Hebrew, this is what to fear the Lord meant – to keep his commandments, to walk in his ways, to listen to his voice, to cling to him, to love him and to serve him.[4] No wonder it is called the beginning of wisdom and the first principle of all knowledge.

3. **We relate to God in the same way that we relate to other people**, which is why problems in relating to God affect our relationships with each other, and problems in our relationships with each other affect our relationship with God.[5]

Our relationship with God and our relationships with each other are essentially similar in nature. Not exactly the same, because there are factors in our relationship with God (worship for example), that are exclusive to him and have no place in human relationships, but otherwise they are essentially of the same order. That is why you might observe that many of the worship songs we sing to Christ could, with minor modification of the words, become love songs we could sing to our wife or husband or sweetheart. And that is also why John in his epistle can say in one place that we know we love God because we love our brothers, and in another place can say we know we love our brothers because we love God.[6] Let us look then at the essential nature of these interactions that lie so close to the core of our humanness.

What are they?

Every day of our life we are involved in contacts and interactions with other people. Some interactions fall into the category of personal relationships but these are of very different kinds. Some, as in marriage or family are private and exclusive, others such as membership of sports clubs or churches or political parties are public and inclusive. Some are fairly permanent and regularly engaged in, for example relationships with colleagues at work, others are irregular and intermittent for example the relationship between doctor and patient or shopkeeper and customer. But what is the common ground that justifies them all being classed as personal relationships? The following simple definition will apply to most of our relationships and expresses their essential nature.

A relationship is the mutual sharing of life between two or more persons

Note that we restrict our definition to relationships between people. Obviously there are other kinds of relationships, for example those between people and animals or between people and their environment but these are outside the scope of our present study.

Several important implications arise from our definition.

1. Mutuality

For a relationship to exist between two persons, each must make some contribution or supply some kind of input into the interaction going on between them. You cannot have a totally one-sided or unilateral relationship, both parties must participate in some way. A member of a fan-club may idolise a movie star, may know intimate details about her life-style, her tastes and her opinions, he may spend most of his spare time running a club to promote her interests, but if he is completely unknown to his idol he does not have a relationship with her in spite of his activity on her behalf.

The contribution made by the parties to a relationship does not have to be the same either in kind or in degree. In a business the worker contributes his time, his skill and his efforts; the employer contributes money, direction and facilities – a relationship exists between them. A teacher contributes her knowledge, her expertise and her enthusiasm for the subject; the pupils contribute their attention, questions, efforts and examination results; there is a relationship between teacher and class. Sometimes one of the parties may seem to do all the giving, for example a mother with her new born baby, but baby makes her contribution to the relationship too, as any mother will tell you.

Mutuality has other implications also. If a relationship is to grow and develop the responsibility to produce that result rests on both parties. If a relationship breaks down you can count on it that there has been failure of some kind on both sides – and if a broken relationship is to be restored, both parties must accept the mutual obligation to work to that end. A relationship never survives unilaterally, almost never breaks down unilaterally and certainly can never be restored unilaterally.

2. Sharing life

When we consider what relating actually consists of we are getting into more sensitive territory. What is it made up of? Is it merely a series of behaviours or outward interactions, or is there something more?

You go into a store and the sales assistant wraps your purchase, takes your money and says, "Thank you." It is like going to a slot machine. You go into another store and the sales assistant wraps your purchase, takes your money and says, "Thank you." You feel welcomed, appreciated, admired; you get the impression that your purchase has made the whole day's work seem worthwhile. I guarantee that is the shop you will want to go back to. What is the difference? One sales assistant put her services into the transaction, the other also put herself. But what does that mean?

The fact is that we are embodied spirit – incarnate spirit might be an even better way of understanding it. Our essential core is spirit. The body without the spirit is dead. It is a corpse, James tells us in his epistle.[7] But because we are spirit, we live off spirit. For example, can you recall the last time you spoke to someone and it was one of those occasions when things really clicked? The vibes were right, you were on the same wavelength, however you want to describe it. Do you remember what it felt like afterwards? You felt alive, exhilarated, excited, somehow fulfilled. What happened was that you touched the other person's spirit. Spirit lives off spirit. Recall the other time you spoke with somebody and that invisible glass wall was between you. All you did was exchange words, mouth platitudes or trade arguments. What did you feel like afterwards? Bored, drained, tired, tense, out of sorts. What happened was that you reached for spirit and were foiled.

Sharing life involves the interaction of spirit. Some people do it readily, naturally their relationships always have life and vibrancy about them. Others do it poorly, or, as was true of me well into mid life, don't know how to do it at all. They often have a deep longing for relationships that mean something but somehow they never manage to pull it off, and they don't know why that is so. Such people have never learned how to reach out in their spirit so that they share themselves with others. It is not a matter of personality or temperament, extroverts versus introverts. An extrovert can perish with inner loneliness in spite of all his noise and talk because he cannot reach people and people cannot reach him. The real person is locked inside the image or hidden behind the role being played. An introvert may slip quietly into the company without being noticed but the first

13

person to speak with her wants thereafter to monopolise her time because he has stumbled on somebody real and somebody who draws him out to be real too. We will come back to this aspect several times in the course of our study.

3. A third entity

Entity may not be the best word to use, but calling it a factor or an element hardly does it justice. The point is that a relationship is a separate entity or reality in its own right, quite apart from the persons who make it up. In a marriage the husband and wife are two entities, but there is also a third entity, the husband/wife relationship. There is the employer and the employee, there is also the employer/employee relationship. In business this is clearly recognised. The work relationship is defined and described in contractual terms, such as conditions of employment, wage awards, job descriptions and so on. But the relationship also includes things like management styles and the attitudes of management and workers towards each other.

It is because the relationship is a reality in its own right that you often observe an astonishing disparity between who the parties are in themselves and what the relationship is between them. I have seen two very ordinary people, of very modest individual capacities and talents and with very little going for them in either looks or personality, but they have a marriage that glows. I have seen other cases where there are two people who individually are exceptionally gifted, charming, kindly and attractive, but their marriage is a walking disaster. The first couple are putting all their modest endowments into their relationship, the second have long since stopped putting anything very much into theirs.

People do not generally understand this seemingly obvious principle or they do not attend to its implications. Many a wife, instead of working on her husband/wife relationship is working on her husband, trying to modify the design if she can. Husbands do the same. Unions and employers waste endless hours and multiplied dollars in similar futile exercises, employers trying to change unionists into free market entrepreneurs, unions trying to convert employers into Fabian socialists. Meanwhile the heart of the matter, the relationship between the parties accumulates failures and unresolved grievances that sometimes stress asunder the whole thing or at best make the relationship unproductive and unsatisfying for both sides.

Our relationship with God

All that we have said so far, and most of what will follow, applies also to our relationship with God. It may even apply primarily to our relationship with him and only after that to our relationship with each other.

The aspect of mutuality means that although God most certainly wants to be actively in relationship with us and has done all that is needed to bring that about, the whole thing will work only if we are prepared to be actively involved with him. More than once God has said to me, "I can do no more with you and take you no further until you do something about improving your personal relationship with Me."

God's contribution is unlimited in its grace and its extent but the quality of the relationship between us depends also on what we put into it, and what we have to put in, is what any relationship necessarily requires – ourselves. I may spend hours in Bible study and prayer and Christian service of different kinds but if I am not personally present in it, if my spirit is not given into it there will be no real relationship with God and I will rapidly become bored with what seems to be meaningless exercises.

But if putting myself into a human relationship means that I touch another human spirit and doing so is so exciting and life giving, what happens when my spirit touches the Holy Spirit of God? That is eternal life, it is the well of living water, that is being plugged into the mains and no mistake!

How do we do it? Simply by giving ourselves wholeheartedly, reaching out in our spirit to God and consciously and continually building a real relationship with him. It is drawing near in our heart to him, being present in our praying and practising his presence. The amazing thing is that God does the same thing towards us.

Reflect on it. Do you notice that although there are six billion people in the world today when you turn to God he never says, "Wait a minute, I'm very busy right now." Nor does he give you one six-billionth part of his attention. In some incredible way he gives you his total undivided attention. That is amazing. Of course while he is giving you his total undivided attention he is also giving me and millions of others his total undivided attention and all at the same time. That is because he is Infinite. In our relationship with God, then, what are we to work on? You've got it, not on God but on the quality of our relating to him, its honesty, its integrity, its faithfulness, its heartiness. How we do that will emerge more clearly as we proceed.

References

1. Genesis 1:26.
2. Genesis 2:18.
3. Ecclesiastes 4:9–12.
4. Deuteronomy 10:12, 13, 20; 13:4.
5. 1 Peter 3:7.
6. 1 John 4:12; 5:2.
7. James 2:26.

Chapter 2

Categories for Understanding Relationships

We have seen that relationships are both possible and normative for man because they are part of God's design for his life from the beginning. But before we go further we need some basic categories that will help us to bridge the gap between our general definition of relationships and the specific types of relationships in which we are involved day by day. These categories involve two fundamental types of relationship and two fundamental dimensions that apply to virtually all relationships. For the first of these we turn to the book of Genesis which records the origin of two quite different kinds of relationship.

1. **Instrumental** or **co-operative** relationships, and
2. **Consummatory** or **social** relationships.

Instrumental relationships

Genesis 1:26–28 is generally called the creation mandate, or the dominion mandate given by God to man in relation to the rest of creation.

> *"Be fruitful and increase in number; fill the earth and subdue it. Rule over the fish of the sea and the birds of the air and over every living creature that moves on the ground."*

The command and the authority are given to man, male and female and multiplied man, that is to humankind as a whole. To steward God's creation is to be a co-operative undertaking in which men and women combine their efforts and resources to do

17

together what they would never be able to accomplish on their own. Note that co-operation, not competition is at the beginning. This type of relationship can also be called *instrumental*, that is, it is a means to an end. Individuals may enter into co-operative relationships to reach a goal, attain an objective, complete a common task, achieve a purpose. The relationship is an instrument to that end and without the existence of the goal or purpose there would be nothing to cause the people to relate. Many of our relationships are of this type, for example those between employer and employee, teacher and pupils, or supplier and customer. It may be true there are also socially rewarding aspects to the relationship but without the task or goal they would not be enough to sustain it in being.

Consummatory relationships

In Genesis 2:18 we have something quite different. God looked at Adam in the Garden of Eden and said:

> *"It is not good for the man to be alone, I will make a helper suitable for him."*

So from Adam's side God fashioned woman and brought her to him. In Adam's ecstatic cry *"Bone of my bones and flesh of my flesh"* we have the institution of a new kind of relationship.

> *"For this reason a man will leave his father and mother and be united to his wife and they will become one flesh."*[1]

Here we have a relationship that is not co-operative but social, it is not instrumental but consummatory, that is, the relationship is not a means to an end, it is an end in itself. This is the beginning of relationships that are "good" in themselves, that is, they need no external goal or purpose to justify their existence. Marriage is not *for* any purpose or end outside the marriage, it is for the sake of being married. Marriage is not even for the sake of having children; it would even be truer to say that children and family are for the sake of completing and fulfilling marriage. What makes divorce so disastrous is that it destroys a God-given end. It is not surprising that when the end or purpose disappears, the means is also called in question. If marriage goes on the rocks what is the point of having children. There is a link between the attitude to abortion in our society and the breakdown of the institution of marriage that has not received the attention it deserves. Recover a biblical view of marriage and see what happens to the abortion rate.

Of course few relationships are purely instrumental or purely consummatory. Even work has an important social aspect and friends and families sometimes join forces for specific tasks and projects. Nevertheless misunderstanding or differing understandings of the essential character of a relationship are very common sources of problems.

For example if I find my friendship is being cultivated because I could be a good support at the committee table for the other person's project, I will feel I am being "used". Friendship is not meant to be a means to an end, in my book at any rate. On the other hand if a salesman calls at my office and then settles down for a cosy chat about his family and his weekend activities I am likely to get irritated because he is "wasting my time". He is there for a purpose and ought to get on with it.

But I would see nothing wrong with a colleague lobbying for my support for a project, or with a friend dropping by the office for a chat. In these cases the nature of the relationship is understood and respected on both sides and there is no sense of it being misused for other ends.

The same distinction requires that I cannot reasonably expect my foreman or my manager to treat me as a buddy and be sensitive to my every need. I must abide by the general terms of the relationship which is primarily an instrumental one and not take it amiss if the emphasis is on quality and productivity and not on social interaction. Confusion over this is often a real issue in Christian businesses or in the management and administrative areas of missions or welfare organisations. Staff relations are important, make no mistake about that, but sometimes I have found people who expect that their managers or supervisors on the job will meet their needs for fellowship, pastoring, counselling, and even teaching and worship within the context of the daily job. But that is not what that particular relationship is really all about. Having said that, I agree that in many areas of Christian work the division between cooperative and social relationships is by no means clear cut. An open, honest, clarification of the ground-rules, would however avoid a lot of unnecessary problems.

Our Godward relationship

Man was made first of all for relationship with God and there are therefore some aspects of that relationship that have no counterpart with his relationships with other human beings. Worship is one; its exclusive object is God alone, to give worship to anyone or anything other than God is idolatry and condemned as such.[2] The primacy of obedience to God over any other human authority is also essential, and it is only when this prior claim has been recognised our other relationships will fall into place.

In many ways, however, the dynamics of our relationship with God are the same as the dynamics of our relationship with other people. **Firstly our relationship with God is the most *instrumental* of all relationships**. It is for a purpose, the most exalted of all purposes, the thing that gripped the heart of Paul so persistently:

> *"I press on to take hold of that for which Christ Jesus took hold of me."*[3]

God's purpose from all eternity is the establishment of his Kingdom, a goal so great that Jesus said it is like treasure hidden in a field. If a man once sees it, he will sell everything he possesses for it. Miss that purpose and all we can reach for is limited to the capacity of our tiny little ego and a lifespan like a weaver's shuttle. The greatest of man's goals become so trivial that men and women wonder if life is really worth the bother, or settle for living on the thin rind of life's surface refusing to think or probe any deeper. I remember speaking to a prominent educator in New Zealand who had retired after reaching the top in his chosen career, and asking him how he was enjoying his new found leisure. I will never forget the look of his face "Tom," he said, "It is terrible. It is like going to the bank and finding all your money has turned to ashes." He was dead within the year.

But when we are caught up in God's magnificent purposes, everything has meaning, and is purposeful. Difficulties and obstacles shrink to insignificant proportions when the Kingdom is involved and the smallest thing has eternal significance if it has to do with the Kingdom.

Make no mistake, God does not need us. He is sovereign and he can do anything he wants anytime he wants. God is omnipotent, therefore he has all the power there is, he is omniscient therefore he has all the knowledge there is, he is eternal, he has all the time there is. You cannot overpower God, you cannot outsmart God, you cannot outlast God. But that is a sovereignty that does not satisfy the heart of God. The only sovereignty that satisfies his heart is the sovereignty of Fatherhood, that is having his purposes accomplished by sons and daughters who do it just because it is the Father's will. That will keep us motivated all our life, and all the life to come.

But our relationship with God is also the most consummatory of all. To know him is the supreme end of all existence. If we know Christ only for the benefits his salvation brings, we do not yet really know him. "Jesus Christ," someone has said, "is so holy and so attractive that if we saw him we would love him even if he was not our Redeemer." Paul understood that also. *"I count everything a loss compared to the surpassing greatness of knowing Christ Jesus my Lord."*[4]

This creates a revolution in our attitudes. To pray – just for the sake of praying, to worship – just to worship God, to serve him for the sheer joy of serving, to read the Bible, just because it is his book, to know him, just for the joy of knowing him.

Amazingly God ascribes these same consummatory qualities to his relationship with us because he chooses to be our friend, in its way probably the most selfless of all human relationships. *"Abraham my friend,"* said God. *"You are my friends,"* said Jesus.[5] There is an equality about friendship; you cannot command a friend so for God to choose such a relationship with created beings is perhaps the most astonishing condescension of all.

How deep, how wide?

There are two other categories that are important in describing personal relationships:

1. **Intimacy or closeness**. How deeply do we intend or expect to enter into each other's life in this relationship?

21

2. **Scope or extent**. How much of our life is to be involved in this relationship?

Relationships vary widely both in the level of intimacy involved and the extent of the interaction. Moreover although intimacy and extent may be directly related to one another that is not necessarily the case. A work relationship or a business partnership can occupy a substantial part of our waking hours and an even greater part of our thought life and yet involve very little personal intimacy. On the other hand a counselling session or a medical consultation can involve a very deep level of intimacy but may touch only a narrow sector of our life and last only a very short space of time.

Intimacy

Differing understanding and expectations as to the intimacy involved in a relationship can be as troublesome as any other aspect. For example if I try to bring into a relationship a level of intimacy that the other person does not expect or desire or allow for, I will appear intrusive, embarrassing and too close for comfort. On the other hand if the other person expects to have deep, intimate sharing of desires, fears and feelings but I do not reciprocate I will seem to them to be stand-offish, aloof and superficial.

Marriage is meant to be the most intimate of all human relationships, so close indeed that it is described as *"becoming one flesh."*[6] But partners coming into a marriage may come with very different ideas on what constitutes intimacy and with very different capacities to share the deep things of their hearts with each other. If these differences are not expressed or understood and if they are not allowed for, there are potential problems looming. The same is true of other areas of family life. As the children grow up, how much can parents assume that they ought to share in all the aspirations, fears, plans and doubts of their teenage or older children? How much of their own agonies, despair and hopes should they share with their children? There are no ready-made or fail-safe answers to these dilemmas. Children often suffer greatly both in childhood and in later life through lack of intimacy between them and their parents. But I have also known people who have been deeply wounded as

22

children because they carried a burden of parental problems and parental confidences far beyond their capacity to bear.

Counsellors, ministers and priests also face potential problems over intimacy with those they counsel. If the person who opened the deep places of her life to you today expects that level of intimacy to continue, while you do not, she may be deeply hurt if she meets you in the supermarket next day and you pass her with a smile and a cheery wave. On the other hand the person who expects the intimacy of the counselling room to end at your study door may tomorrow wonder if he has told you too much if you go out of your way to inquire into his state, instead of passing with a smile and a cheery wave.

A great potential for problems arises when the question of the agreed level of intimacy has never been addressed or discussed. There is much to be gained from setting the ground-rules clearly at the beginning of the relationship so that both parties understand what is expected or acceptable. This need not set the relationship in concrete. Relationships are dynamic, not static, and they are always changing, but intimacy is such a sensitive issue it should never be taken for granted.

Here are some of the important considerations that affect the matter of intimacy in relationships.

1. The motivation for intimacy is the desire to become one with another while still retaining our own identity

When the desire is to become one with God we are seeking bliss, when it is to become one with another person, we are seeking love, and when it is to become one with a group we are seeking community. In all these experiences, the retention of our identity and individuality are all-important. Union with God does not mean being absorbed in the Divine, it is becoming his sons and daughters;[7] a marriage where one partner totally dominates the other is pathological and a community where people lose their identity in the group becomes a cult.

2. We have a created need for intimacy, because only intimacy has the capacity to end our loneliness

One of the most remarkable statements in Scripture is made about Adam. Concerning Adam in his unfallen state, and Adam in the Garden of Eden God said, *"It is not good for the man to be alone.*"[8] Man needs intimacy with his own kind, so the woman is taken out of man to provide that intimacy for both. In the shared intimacy of a close relationship we touch the spirit of each other and at the deepest level of our being we are no longer alone, but received, affirmed, loved and given life.

3. Intimacy creates vulnerability because the walls are down between us and the emotions are always involved

In intimacy we are not only open to love and affirmation, we are also open to the possibility of hurt because what we share or reveal can be misunderstood or used against us. We also run the risk of rejection if the intimacy that is offered or sought is spurned. Furthermore because the emotions are always involved in an intimate relationship, a breakdown is always very painful and can be emotionally devastating.

4. For intimacy to thrive requires a committed relationship

The nature of the link between intimacy and commitment needs to be clearly understood. You can have relationships where there is real commitment without there necessarily being any great measure of intimacy between the parties. This is often the case with relationships based on commitment to a common cause or goal. On the other hand, because intimacy produces vulnerability it requires commitment for its security. This is true even in relationships where intimacy is specialised and temporary, for example a counselling situation. Only if clients are convinced that a counsellor is sincerely committed to their welfare will they take the risk of disclosing intimate details of their life and problems.

The tragedy today is that people are so hungry for intimacy yet so afraid of commitment that they seek intimacy in uncommitted relationships and time and again reap devastating hurt.

5. In relationships we swing emotionally between two desires, a desire for intimacy and a desire for privacy

Both these needs or desires should be recognised as right and natural, the need to be very close to someone and the need to be on our own. In fact only where privacy is also respected can real intimacy flourish. Normally we swing emotionally between the two poles, and sensitivity is required because one partner's desire for intimacy may be at the very time the other partner needs privacy. Unless we are aware of what is really happening we will read rejection into one response, or intrusiveness and domination into the other.

6. You cannot be equally intimate with a large number of people

This is a very important principle in church fellowships where one of the problems is that we model only two types of relationship, one very close and the other very distant. We need to realise that there is a whole range of valid and worthwhile relationships that have very different degrees of intimacy.

Jesus had two groups of disciples, the 72 and the 12. He was much more intimate with the 12 than he was with the 72, and even within the twelve he had three with whom he was particularly close. He took Peter, James and John to places that he did not take the other nine and he shared things with them that he did not share with the rest. Even amongst the three, there was one who was especially intimate, John, the disciple who *"lay back on Jesus breast."* [9]

The tabernacle in the wilderness gives us a useful model for understanding relationships. Basically it had three main areas:
(a) The Outer Court into which any Hebrew could come
(b) The Holy Place, where only the priests could enter, and
(c) The Holy of Holies, where only the High Priest could enter.

We all have people who for us belong in the outer court, that is, there are relationships but no real intimacy is involved. There is a smaller circle who belong in our holy place and fewer still, perhaps only half a dozen in our whole life, who are intimate enough to belong in the holy of holies. If someone who belongs in the outer court tries to crash into the holy place, we are entitled to hang up a "No Go" sign. If they try to crash into the holy of holies we had better hang up a "No Go" sign, because in neither case is the relationship going to work. Wisdom and grace are obviously needed in handling the situation because the person desiring intimacy is certainly going to feel rejected, but the trauma is going to be even worse later on, unless the matter of appropriate intimacy is properly adjusted in the beginning.

25

Scope or extent

1. The problem of undiscussed assumptions

In work situations the nature and extent of relationships is generally carefully defined in a job description or a union award, but in voluntary associations, such as churches, or in social relationships it is rarely specified. Indeed because even work relationships have a social aspect the same issues arise over how far a particular relationship is meant to extend. For example does my relationship with a professional colleague necessarily mean that I have to be his confidante for all his family problems or do I have to listen to a blow by blow description of how he broke par on the golf course at the weekend. He obviously assumes so, but do I? Should I in turn regale him with my analysis of the Brahmns symphony I listened to last night even although I know he is tone deaf? Where do the legitimate limits of the foreman's interest in his staff lie? When does he cease to be a caring supervisor and become a nosey parker? In how much of the private lives of all my congregation am I expected to participate? Am I meant to be at the beck and call of that alcoholic husband or that compulsive talker any hour of the day or night?

Difficulties arise often in a marriage and the culprit is again undiscussed assumptions. A wife, for example, may assume that because in their marriage they are one, they should share everything with each other. Thus when her husband comes home she gives him a detailed account of all her day and all the children's goings-on. Furthermore she expects her husband to share about what went on in the factory that day. If he does not do so she may feel shut out of an important part of her husband's life, or she may have an uneasy suspicion that he is actually hiding things from her. The husband on the other hand may merely assume that work is work and as such ceases at 5 p.m. He sees no merit in bringing it home to clutter up his evening. He has come home to get away from all that, and anyway what is the point of rehearsing what he did today, he will do the same things tomorrow, and the day after. If his wife presses him for details he may get first irritated, then defensive, then resentful because her unspoken suspicion is starting to show.

It is not so much that one approach as to what should be shared is right and the other wrong, or even that one is better than the other, it is that the two people have different perspectives on the matter but have never put their assumptions up for discussion.

2. The scope or extent of relationships also deals with the question of boundaries

All of us are involved in numerous different relationships each demanding or claiming rights over a certain amount of our time and attention, our commitment and loyalty, our support and our maney. For example we may owe loyalty to our employer, to the church, to our marriage and family, our sports club, a community service association and a political party.

Problems of competing demands and competing loyalties arise at the boundaries or the interface between different relationships. For example on a particular Wednesday evening, the school PTA, a backlog of paper work from the office, the monthly deacons meeting and my wife's need for company and comfort may all be clamouring for my presence. In order to reduce conflict as far a possible it is important that the boundaries of obligations and priorities between relationships are clearly established and understood by all concerned.

Intimacy with God?

We cannot leave the subject without reminding ourselves that the questions of intimacy and scope also apply supremely to our relationship with God. In fact it is the relationship that we have with the Holy Spirit that is the most intimate of all relationships. The closest two human beings can come is fellowship or the one flesh of marriage. The relationship of the Holy Spirit with our spirit is a relationship of 'in-being' or mutual indwelling, we are in him and he is in us. *"He that is joined to the Lord is one spirit with the Lord."*[10] But true as that may be as to our state is it true in our experience – or is it reserved for only a few to know real intimacy with the Creator? Can we cultivate it, and is it really available to us? Let me say this – intimacy at any level is hard won and not without pain. In fact growth and development at any level involves pain and suffering. Athletes soon learn they have to pay the price and push through the pain level to improve their performance or win the race. In the same way we have to pay the price and push through the pain level if we are to grow

27

emotionally, spiritually and relationally. That sits uneasily with our soft modern ethos and our gospels of healing and prosperity and constant overcoming. But it is true to life and to Scripture nevertheless. Pain is something we try to avoid if we possibly can. But we do not avoid it; instead we settle for the pain of unfit bodies or distorted emotional responses or relational loneliness.

The same is true about the scope or extent of our relationship with God. It embraces everything, whatever we do, whether in word or in deed, we are to do it all in the name of the Lord Jesus as the expression of our thankfulness to God the Father.[11]

My friend Wyn Fountain in New Zealand made the point as effectively as any in a book he wrote a few years ago called *The Other Hundred Hours*. This was his startling thesis:

Each week we live 7×24 hours   = 168 hours
If we sleep 8 hours a night, 7×8 =   56 hours
Our time awake each week   = 112 hours

Then he said this – the average earnest Christian cannot possibly spend much more than 12 hours a week at church meetings or religious exercises of one kind or another. Taking the 12 away from the 112 leaves 100 hours a week which we spend in various ways on non-religious activities. **What is God's concern about those other hundred hours?**

Of course God is concerned about them; he is concerned about everything we do. But if Wyn is right and we spend something like 90% of our time on purely secular activities, it must mean that 90% of God's time, he also is concerned about secular things. Life is divided structurally between the spiritual and the secular but they are equally important to God. The spiritual is our worship in the sanctuary, the secular is our service in the world; worship and service always go together – *"Worship the Lord your God and serve him only."*[12]

The building blocks of relationships

We come now to the elements that are necessary to build a relationship with someone else and to maintain it in life and health. Mutual participation there must be, but of itself that is not enough. The same can be said of having a common interest or a joint purpose. Important as these are, they are not sufficient on their own to guarantee the success, let alone the survival of a relationship. Many marriages, business partnerships or political alliances start out with all of these but peter out or blow apart further down the track. There has to be more than compatability or common goals.

All relationships of whatever kind consist of four basic elements or factors. They constitute the basic building blocks. Other things may be involved, may even be very important, these four, however, are essential. If any of them are neglected or adversely affected the relationship will come under stress. If the failure is not addressed or corrected, the relationship will begin to break down.

The four factors or elements we will examine are:

1.   Love – the most enduring
2.   Trust – the most fragile
3.   Respect or honour – the most neglected, and
4.   Understanding or knowledge – the one that takes longest

The relative importance of these elements may differ in different relationships. In the relationship between followers and leaders, trust may be the dominant element, between employers and employee it may be respect, between members of a family it may be love. Nevertheless all four are essential in every relationship and none can be neglected without serious consequences. Similarly the way in which they are expressed may vary. Love between husband and wife is expressed differently from love between friends or love between teacher and pupils, but it has to be there, in every relationship.

Furthermore the elements are no substitutes for one another. You cannot compensate for failure in one area by extra attention to another. You cannot say I don't trust him, but I still love him. Love will not make up for mistrust. You cannot say I have lost respect for her but I still really understand her. Understanding will not make up for disrespect. Relationships were made to stand solidly on four legs, if one is weak they will wobble, if two go they will undoubtedly collapse. To build an enduring relationship we need therefore to know what we have to do in each of the four areas. In addition we have to put that knowledge to use, consistently and persistently until it becomes our natural way of functioning.

References

1. Genesis 2:24.
2. Exodus 20:3–5.
3. Philippians 3:12.
4. Philippians 3:8.
5. Isaiah 41:8; John 15:14.
6. 1 Corinthians 6:16.
7. 2 Corinthians 6:18.
8. Genesis 2:18.
9. John 21:20.
10. 1 Corinthians 6:17.
11. Colossians 3:17.
12. Luke 4:8.

Chapter 3

Love, the Enduring One

We begin with the question of love, not because it is necessarily the most important element but because our very familiarity with it and emphasis on it often innoculates us against its real significance.

We make two common and serious errors of judgment as to the place of love in personal relationships. One is that we do not give it place at all in some relationships, such as those in the marketplace of business and commerce for example, and the other is that we expect it to carry the whole burden in other relationships such as marriage and parenting. "If we just love one another enough everything will work out fine." As we will see, we are wrong in both assumptions.

Part of the problem may be that in our language "love" has become such an omnibus word that it has virtually lost all meaning. I may say at different times I "love" my wife, I love Siamese cats, I love fishing, God, brass band music, Italian cooking and crossword puzzles. The question then is, how in fact do I love my wife? In the same way as I love pizzas or cryptic crosswords? Love as a word turns out to be heavily depreciated currency.

Out of all that you may have read or heard on the subject of love let us distill some basic principles that may help us to get a handle on it. The truth is that while we are told often enough that we must love, preachers seldom tell us how to do it.

Firstly, we must distinguish between emotional love and volitional love. Emotional love is a matter of the feelings or affections. I may be aroused to tenderness at the sight of a small child, to romantic feelings in the presence of a beautiful woman, to compassion, which is love and sorrow, at the sight of a person in need and so on. Such feeling states are always by-products, that is to say they are psychic responses to events or happen ings that take place in our environment and to which we are exposed. They are important; our emotions are part of our God-given endowment as persons. They are motivators or psychic motors, that is, they move us. The word emotion comes from the Latin *movere*, to move. But because the emotions are responses they are in themselves morally valueless. The feelings of "love" for example can lead us into lust as easily as into marital devotion.

The emotions are meant to power our behaviour but they are unreliable themselves for deciding what our behaviour ought to be. The feelings of tenderness or even compassion can become pleasant states that we savour for their own sake. When that happens they degenerate into mere sentimentalism. The emotions are meant to move us, they were never meant to be an end in themselves.

The other kind of love is volitional love, that is it involves a response of our will or active choice. It is this intentional choice that gives love its moral value. I *can* choose to love. That is why God says, *"You shall love the Lord your God,"*[1] or *"love your enemies."*[2] If love is purely a matter of feelings how can I possibly love God unless I feel loving towards him, and how on earth can I feel loving to someone who has just stolen my car or blackened my wife's good name?

Love is actually a response that is meant to engage all our faculties. God who is love and therefore the author and beginner of it has laid down the parameters of love very clearly, although I doubt whether we realise the significance of the statement. To love, God says, is to do it with *"all your heart, with all your soul, with all your mind and with all your strength."*[3] Love that is only a matter of warm feelings is mere sentiment, love that engages only our mind is only admiration, and love that is only a matter of will is charity in its cold, negative sense. We may say then that love has the essential attributes of an attitude, that is, there is a cognitive or intellectual element, there is also an emotional or feeling element and there is also a behavioural element. A loving attitude is what counts in relationships.

Secondly we have to realise the extreme significance of loving God first. It is not that God wants to be king of the castle or top of the popularity poll but it is only when we love God first that we can properly and freely love other people. The reality of our created nature is that we were made for divine love. We have a created need to be loved with a love that is totally dependable and eternally changeless. We have a deep longing for the security of being loved, for ourselves and for no other reason, not for what we can do, or give, or achieve, but just for ourselves. Only God can love like that. Only God loves out of fulness and not out of need. Only He loves us for ourselves alone. Only his love is as changeless as himself. Unless however, our need for that kind of love is satisfied by God's love we will go looking for it from people, and none of them can provide it, not lover, friend, wife, parent or brother. We lay impossible burdens on marriage, friendships or other relationships to provide us with divine love.

Furthermore we have an instinctive sense of the supreme value of love so that we want to invest our love only on somebody who is totally worthy of it and somebody who will live up to all our ideals as a worthy object. But only one person will never let us down. That is Christ. We can love him with all our heart, mind, soul and strength and never be disappointed by flaws in his character or defects in his behaviour. If however we do not invest our love on God we look for standards of performance in return for love, that no human person can possibly attain. We say, or convey to our husband, or our children, "I love you so much you must never disappoint me or let me down." Impossible. They never took on an assignment like that nor do they have any hope of meeting such requirements.

The marvellous thing is that when we love God first and before all, then our need for divine, unchanging love is satisfied. It is then that our need for a perfect person to love is met and we are set free to give and receive what human love can give and receive – variable, up and down, all-over-the-place, warm, passionate, friendly, affectionate, caring human love and response. Great stuff, but like ourselves, vastly less than perfect.

Putting content into love

The Bible, by far the best handbook on the market about loving, is very rich in terms and concepts that express the dynamic and wholehearted nature of love. Some of them are more affective states like sympathy or compassion or tenderness or pity, others like care or concern or kindness emphasise more the active expression of love. Let us examine some of the more important of these terms.

Care – love in action

The essential characteristic of care is that it has to be expressed in behaviour. You cannot say "I care" and then do nothing. The complaint so often heard in relationships that are supposed to be loving ones is, "You don't care," or "Nobody cares," and that is usually exactly what is wrong with the relationship. Substitute "care" for "love" in some of the best known scriptures on the subject and it lights them up in a new way. For example, *"God so cared for the world that he gave his only begotten Son . . . "*;[4] *"We care because he first cared for us"*;[5] *"This is care . . . that God cared for us and sent his Son as an atoning sacrifice for our sins"*.[6]

Care is the key test for the presence of love in a relationship and its pervasiveness underlines the extent of our need for it. It is love at its widest reach, doctors and nurses who care for their patients, schools that care about their pupils, local councillors who care about their districts. No business will ever succeed that does not care for its staff or care about its products or care about its customers. Care, like neighbourly love is not a matter of having warm affectionate feelings towards people, it is about attending to their welfare and best interests as faithfully and as consistently as we attend to our own. Mutual care leads to harmony and fruitful interaction. Whenever it is neglected, or we become care-less, the result is strife, contention and inefficiency.

Kindness – love and fellow-feeling

Love is always kind because that is its very nature.[7] The roots of kindness lie in the deep sense of our kin-ship with one another, in other words it is *"brotherly-kindness"*.[8] The fact that God is kind to us even in our fallenness,[9] carries with it the recognition that we are actually his next-of-kin, indeed the Hebrew word for God as our Redeemer,[10] *ge'ol*, literally means "the one who acts as kinsman".

When we are kind there is also an intuitive feeling that what we are doing is the sort of thing that in similar circumstances we would want somebody else to do for us, therefore what we do is gratuitous or free. Because of this sense of fellow-feeling, kindness is very closely linked to sympathy,[11] and to mercy or compassion.[12]

Unkindness is hurtful precisely because it breaches or wounds this sense of kinship and leaves us feeling somehow rejected and alienated.

Liking – love at its most pleasant

Liking often seems a somewhat superficial and ephemeral response over which we have little control. We say, you have to love people, but you don't have to like them. Liking, however, plays an enormously important part in all relationships where any degree of intimacy is involved, and indeed it is one of the main factors that draws us towards intimacy. On the other hand to be intimately involved with a person whom you dislike can be unbearable.

Liking is one of the most pleasurable aspects of love. It expresses the enjoyment and delight we find in each other's person or presence or company. In the Bible it is called *"finding favour in your sight"*.[13] Liking is made up of attraction, appeal, interest, affection, fondness and other agreeable or favourable reactions or responses. It probably arises at first from the ways in which different personalities, or different sexes stimulate or complement one another and it grows from the mutual exchange and interaction in a loving relationship.

Friendship – love at its most disinterested

The special qualities of friendship need to be appreciated more and understood better particularly amongst Christians. We have a particular vocation to be friends, to be friends to the friendless and the sinners as Jesus was.[14] The offer of friendship is hard to resist but people want to be treated as friends, not as evangelistic prospects.

The Bible rates friendship very high, so high indeed that most of what passes for friendship in our modern society is pallid in comparison. It is doubtful if much of it ever gets beyond the level of acquaintanceship.

Firstly, there is an equality about the love of friends. They are consciously and deliberately on the same level as far as their relationship is concerned. That is perhaps why friendship is often so difficult for leaders. They have to get down off their pedestal, abandon the prerogatives of their position and drop the status symbols if they are going to give and receive friendship. I remember the wail of a man trying to establish a friendship with his neighbour who was a minister. He said, "I've tried to be his friend but every time we get together he wants to pastor me or counsel me." Where husbands and wives are true friends, the conflict over headship and what that means in a marriage becomes in practice meaningless. Who ever argued between friends as to who has the final say, or who is boss?

It is this aspect of equality that makes God's choice of friendship as one of the models of relating to us so staggering. *"Abraham my friend"*[15] says God and comes down to talk to him just as he talked to Moses, face to face as a man talks to his friend.[16] Who can imagine what it must have been like when Jesus sat amongst the twelve and called them friends?[17] You cannot command a friend, you cannot exact obedience from a friend. What a friend does is his or her free choice for your sake and your friendship's sake.

Secondly, because of that equality there is a familiarity and an openness granted to friends. They have access to our lives so that they do not need to stand on ceremony or wait for an invitation. Nor do we have to dress up or put on an act with them. Pretense on the one hand and flattery on the other are things that friendship cannot abide. The very disinterestedness of a friend's regard for us requires him to speak the truth at all costs. In this, friends often occupy a unique position – they are close enough to be emotionally sensitive to our feelings but they are distant enough and objective enough to be blunt when that is needed. *"Faithful are the wounds of a friend." "As iron sharpens iron so a man sharpens the face of his friends."*[18] You can almost feel the writer wince as he pens the words.

Finally, the love of a true friend has qualities of endurance almost beyond belief – David and Jonathan, Ittai the Philistine, and King David, Ruth and Naomi. *"Greater love has no man than this,"* said Jesus, *"that a man will lay down his life for his friends."*[19] What is underlined here is the moral obligation of friendship that nothing in life or death itself, must be allowed to separate me from my friend. In the Incarnation Jesus took upon himself the moral obligation of friendship towards us, that is, never to leave us and never to forsake us. For this he died and rose again from the dead; for this he sent his Spirit to unite with our spirit so that now we can cry with the apostle Paul that nothing can separate from the love of God that is in Christ Jesus our Lord, not life or death, or angels or principalities or powers, nor things present or things to come or any other created reality.[20]

Tenderness – love at its gentlest

Tenderness is another expression of love that is closely connected with intimacy, for example, in the relationship of mother to infant, or husband to wife or parent to child. It is evoked in the stronger party by the realisation that the weaker party is very vulnerable and at the same time very precious. Thus God's responses towards us are described as his *"tender mercy"*.[21] and we are therefore to be tender-hearted in our forgiveness of one another.[22]

Tenderness is undemanding, seeking no response or return but asking only to be allowed to give. It is also very gentle, both in word and action because it is aware of the fragility of the one towards whom it is directed, and of the sensitivity of their feelings.[23] For example, in comforting the grieving or calming the troubled or fearful, *"speaking tenderly"* to them is essential,[24] that is to say, the tone of the voice is all important.

Western masculine stereotyping has tended to regard tenderness as somewhat soft and weak, an error that has had disastrous consequences. In countless relationships men have been unable to give or receive tenderness and both they and their wives and children have suffered dreadfully thereby. Although tenderness is gentle it does not, and cannot flow from weakness but only from strength, therefore it is both protective and reassuring and it makes the one who receives it, whether infant, child, wife or friend, feel both secure and cherished.

Generosity – love at its most liberal

This is not just liberality with money, but more importantly, generosity with things like time, attention, assistance, encouragement and praise. It is also manifested in the genuine expression of joy and pleasure in another person's success or good fortune.

It is God's nature to give generously, and extravagantly[25] and we must do the same.[26] Generosity, we discover, is both the key to prosperity and the purpose of prosperity,[27] but this prosperity is also, and even primarily, prosperity of the soul, rich in contents, strength and gifts. Thus the cluster of words that describe generosity, for example, unselfish, open-handed, magnanimous, large hearted, ungrudging, liberal and benevolent could well be the pen portrait of the truly great person or great leader. They suggest largeness of vision, breadth of benevolence and sympathies and wideness of interests.

Compassion – love and sympathy

Compassion, or what sometimes passes for it, often suffers from being mere sentiment; we are aroused by someone's plight, but we do not actually do anything about it. Robert Greenleaf warns about this when he suggests that "Caring compassion is often found in inverse proportion to the ideals of the institution."

Compassion is the feeling of pity or distress at the ills or suffering of others. It requires an imaginative identification with the others" experience and the ability to feel what they are going through. With God, compassion is linked with grace, forgiveness and tenderness,[28] and in Christ it moved him towards meeting the needs of sufferers or the lost.[29] In Paul's epistles it is linked with kindness, humility, gentleness, patience, forgiveness and forbearance.[30]

Compassion is also a kind of litmus paper test as to which emotions are permissible to us as Christians and which are not. If the emotion we feel towards someone is compatible with compassion, then the emotion may well be legitimate, but if it is not compatible with compassion, it is certainly not legitimate. For example, it is possible to feel anger towards a person but still feel compassion towards them; it is not possible to feel malice and compassion towards a person at the same time.

Forgiveness – love at its most gracious

No relationship will survive, let alone flourish, without the willingness to forgive. Forgiveness is ceasing to blame and letting the offending party go free of punishment, recrimination and censure. Forgiveness is a matter of grace because the forgiver gives something up, and in doing so he makes an end of the matter, once and for all.

In relationships we are always in danger of keeping a scorecard in our minds of people's wrongdoings, failures and deficiencies, ready to be used in evidence against them whenever the need arises. If that is so, there has been no real forgiveness. An enormous amount of stress in relationships comes from this kind of unforgiveness and from people feeling that the failures of the past are still being held against them. God's forgiveness maintains no record of our sins, they are never remembered against us any more,[31] and our forgiveness of each other must be the same.[32]

Love's expression

Love is dynamic, that is it has to have an object. You cannot just love, or just have love, you have to love something or somebody. Similarly love needs to be expressed. For children it needs to be expressed many times and in many ways for it to be believable. I have lost count of the number of those who, looking back on their childhood have said sadly "I guess my parents loved me, in their own way, but I never felt it."

Love needs to be spoken out. "I love you" are still the sweetest sounding words we ever hear. A friend of mine had two teenage sons who had been giving him all sorts of bother. He said, "I got them together one day. I felt a bit of a Charlie about it because they were big fellows, but I said to them 'Look I haven't told you this for a long time but I just want you both to know I really love you.'" His conflict with his sons stopped overnight.

Love is also communicated in non-verbal ways, in the way we look at one another, in the way we touch. One of my sons taught at a school where many of the children came from broken homes. He told me how walking the playground in the lunchbreak little children from the primer classes would come up to him and take his hand, not saying anything just walking with him holding hands. After a while they would go off contentedly to play; they had drawn something they needed from the contact of a caring hand.

The more intimate the relationship, the more important does the factor of love become and the more the emotional aspect comes to the surface. This is particularly true of marriage and family because the closer people get to us the more our feelings are engaged in the relationship.

In this connection I note that the injunction to love is given in Scripture more often to the husband than to the wife. There is probably a very good reason for this. Women are responders; love your wife properly and she is unlikely to have much difficulty in loving you enough in return. Be that as it may, the responsibility to see that there is enough love in the marriage clearly rests on the husband. Paul goes further, he says the responsibility on the husband is nothing less than producing a perfect wife! *"Husbands love your wife, even as Christ loved the church and gave himself for her that he might present her to himself a perfect church without spot or wrinkle or any such thing."*[33] As a husband I am under instructions to give myself for my wife so as to provide an environment within which she can be totally fulfilled.

The wider the reach of the relationship, the less important do the affective components of love become and the more important its volitional aspects become. But it is still love. I can report only my own experience here but the truth is, I never ever have warm gushy feelings about myself. When I look at my face in the bathroom mirror in the morning I never go weak at the knees and gasp in rapture "Oh you lovely man!" Never. Yet I notice that I take very good care of myself and attend very faithfully to my needs in spite of my lack of feeling, even when in fact I do not feel good about myself at all. That is the way I am to love my neighbour – the way I love myself, to care for his best interest as faithfully and as conscientiously as I do my own.

References

1. Deuteronomy 6:5.
2. Matthew 5:44.
3. Deuteronomy 6:5; Matthew 22:37.
4. John 3:16.
5. 1 John 4:19.
6. 1 John 4:10.
7. 1 Corinthians 13:4.
8. 2 Peter 1:7.
9. Luke 6:35.
10. Isaiah 60:16.
11. 1 Peter 3:8 ASB.
12. Micah 6:8.
13. Ruth 2:13; Esther 2:9.

14. Matthew 11:19.
15. Isaiah 41:8.
16. Exodus 33:11.
17. John 15:15.
18. Proverbs 27:6, 17 ASB.
19. John 15:13 ASB.
20. Romans 8:29–30.
21. Luke 1:78.
22. Ephesians 4:32 RSV.
23. Isaiah 42:3.
24. Isaiah 40:1–2.
25. James 1:5; Malachi 3:10.
26. Romans 12:8.
27. Proverbs 11:25; 2 Corinthians 9:11.
28. Exodus 34:6; Daniel 9:9; Philippians 2:2.
29. Mark 1:41; Matthew 9:36.
30. Colossians 3:12.
31. Psalm 130:3–4; Jeremiah 31:34.
32. Ephesians 4:32.
33. Ephesians 5:25–27 ASB.

Chapter 4

Trust – the Cost of Commitment

Trust is essential to any life in society since social interaction and social intercourse would be impossible in a world where nobody could be trusted. We need a dependable and predictable environment to be able to order our life with reasonable confidence, therefore we expect the world and the people in it to be trustworthy. A baby is born trusting. Suspicion and mistrust are things it learns later and they are always painful experiences. They change the innocent trust of childhood into the wary eyes that watch us out of so many faces. But although trust is so essential, its nature and its requirements are by no means well known. We call it faith and publish hundreds of books every year to extol its virtues and try to explain its dynamics. It is, nevertheless worth our while to get some clarity on what it actually is before we get too far in our discussion of its role in personal relationships. To do so we will have to get beyond the slogans, religious and otherwise, "Have faith" "Trust me" "only believe" "You can bet your life on it" and so on.

What is trust? What are its conditions? How do you build it? What happens when it is breached or lost? These are basic but vital questions whose answers we cannot assume or take for granted.

Defining trust

Let us begin by attempting a simple definition of trust.

> **Trust is a condition in which you voluntarily make yourself dependent on another person for some outcome or other, or for some result or consequence.**

Note the following important characteristics of the situation we have defined as trust.

1. Trust is a choice you make

You cannot be forced to trust. If you are going to trust someone or put your faith in them, you must do it voluntarily. If people are told by their leaders, "You will just have to trust us in this," the one thing you can be sure of is that they won't trust them even if they have no option but to leave the matter in the leaders' hands.

2. Trust is an attitude

The things that determine the way we live and behave are our attitudes. Attitudes are more than beliefs because beliefs are purely cognitive and people do not generally live by their beliefs. Trust as an attitude has three elements:

(a) *A cognitive element*, that is, it is a belief. You are convinced in your mind that the other person is trustworthy. Abraham, for example, was *"fully persuaded that God had power to do what he had promised."*[1]

(b) *An emotional element* – you feel assurance or confidence in trusting the other person. *"Faith is being sure of what we hope for and certain of what we do not see."*[2]

(c) *A behavioural element* – you act on it. *"Faith without deeds is useless."*[3]

3. Trust is a risk you take

The risk you take when you trust, is that you let certain outcomes in your life go out of your control and into the hands of the person or persons on whose ability and trustworthiness you have chosen to rely. To say that you trust someone to do something and then to do it yourself, or to personally supervise their activities, may get the job done, but it makes nonsense of your claims to trust.

4. The proof that you trust is that you make no contingency plans in case the other person lets you down

To set up a fall-back position or "hedge your bets" so as to provide against a possible let down, may be admirable discretion but it certainly calls into question the level of your trust. If the other person learns of your contingency plans they will soon realise that you don't really trust them at all.

5. The cost of trust is vulnerability

To trust involves taking a position of vulnerability because now the outcome or the consequences are out of my direct control and in the hands of someone else on whose ability or faithfulness I have to rely. It is this state of dependence which trust creates that we find hardest to handle. The heart of our fallenness is our refusal to live in dependence on God. We have deliberately chosen to be independent, to seek self sufficiency, to control our own destiny. Trust strikes at the root of all of these.

But there is also a paradox here. I stumbled across it one time when I was reflecting on how difficult it is to make an ethical case against gambling that is both convincing and appealing. Then I suddenly saw what gambling is, a social evil all right but also a kind of secularised form of faith. It answers to man's need somehow and somewhere in his life to live at risk. Because man has refused to accept the risk of depending on God he has to get his thrills in all sorts of inappropriate and harmful ways. We are created, it seems, with two great needs, the need for certainty and the need for uncertainty. Our need for certainty and security is met by a God who is always the same and whose love and whose word are totally reliable and unchanging. Our need for uncertainty is met by a God who is always doing new things, *"Behold I will do something new among you."*[4] He is continually calling us out of the familiar into the walk of faith, into a personal relationship trusting dependence. Almost against our will, the need for that faith walk, the need for trust, the need for uncertainty, the need for risk insists on surfacing. It explains what Paul meant when he wrote, *"Abraham believed God and it was counted to him for righteousness."*[5] One of the meanings of righteousness is conformity to the norm or standard. When Abraham trusted God, when he took the risk of believing in the promise, without even a son to his name (calculate the odds on that), he conformed to the norm of what man was meant to be, a God-believing being.

The self-sufficiency Adam sought never was and never is possible, so we are forced every day of our lives to choose to trust. This is true of even the simplest things like buying a packet of breakfast cereal or getting on a bus or going into a telephone box to make a call. What is true in these relatively mundane matters is much more the case in personal relationships. In fact, the more important the relationship, the more vital a part trust plays in it. The more intimate the relationship the more trust lies at its very heart and the more costly the commitment of real trust becomes. It is no surprise therefore that trust becomes the dominant issue in critical relationships such as leadership, professional services and public offices on the one hand and intimate relationships like marriage, therapy and counselling on the other.

6. To be trusted is a responsibility you must voluntarily accept

You cannot expect someone to be trustworthy in a particular matter unless they know and agree to the terms of the trust and accept the responsibility to fulfil it. Conscious and deliberate trust has to be matched by conscious and deliberate trustworthiness; conscious and deliberate faith has to be matched by conscious and deliberate faithfulness. *"It is required that those who have been given a trust must prove faithful."*[6]

7. The person who would trust must also himself be trustworthy

It is important to understand why this is necessarily the case. Firstly, if I am going to trust a person, it requires that they take seriously their duty to be reliable and faithful. But they are unlikely to take on such possibly onerous obligations towards me if they discover that for my part I do not take such obligations seriously at all. Secondly, if I do not take trustworthiness seriously myself, I will find it very hard to believe that anyone else will do so and therefore I will have great difficulty in trusting anybody.

The neglected key to growing in faith therefore turns out to be growing in faithfulness. When we become meticulous about keeping our promises we will find it much easier to believe that God is meticulous about keeping his.

8. Accepting trust involves accountability

If I am trusted, and have accepted that trust, I am accountable, that is, I am answerable for the outcome and responsible for any failure. Leadership is a position of trust because people have placed their trust in the leaders. The question then is, to whom are leaders accountable? The answer – they are accountable to all those who have trusted them, and that includes their followers. Many Christian leaders fail to realise this and some would deny it, but trust always involves accountability.

9. Trust once broken is very difficult to restore
Trust differs from other virtues in its extreme fragility. Once trust is broken it is very, very difficult to restore and it always takes time. Forgiveness can be the work of a moment but restoration of confidence and the willingness to trust again is not the work of a moment, it may need patient rebuilding.

A person may act unlovingly on occasion but we will still believe that they are essentially loving, they may do us an unkindness and we will still believe that they are basically kindhearted. But if we trust someone and they let us down, we are likely to have a question mark about their trustworthiness for a long time to come.

One reason for this has to do with the all-or-nothing nature of trust. You either trust or you don't, you cannot partly trust, or if you do, the uncertainty created causes extreme discomfort. Similarly, when trust is broken it is never partially broken, if it is broken at all it is totally broken.

Another is the vulnerability involved in trust, which is always costly, emotionally and psychologically even if in no other way. When trust is broken our supposedly dependable universe is suddenly seen to be unreliable and unpredictable and this causes fear and anxiety which in turn results in the protective emotion of anger towards the cause.

The content of trust

To increase our understanding of trust and trustworthiness we will examine some of the qualitites and character traits that surround the concepts and help to give them substance.

Confidence – trust at its most assured
Confidence is heart trust, it is trust that has been proved right so often that it has come to a state of settled conviction or assurance regardless of what the issue is, or what the circumstances look

like. In the most adverse and dangerous situations, David's confidence in God was unshakeable, because repeated acts of confirmed trust had produced an attitude of complete confidence in God's trustworthiness.[7] So also Paul could say of the Corinthians, *"I have great confidence in you; I take great pride in you."*[8]

Confidence like this depends on our knowledge of a person's character, that is, the way in which their behaviour is governed by, and consistent with ethical and spiritual principles, regardless of the circumstances. To put confidence in an unprincipled person is sheer recklessness.

Confidence is essential for intimacy to blossom. We confide personal and private matters only to those we can trust, therefore it lies at the very heart of the most intimate of our relationships.[9] When that trust is misplaced the consequences can be devastating, we feel not merely let down, we feel betrayed.[10]

Loyalty – trustworthiness at its most committed

The more difficult or dangerous or desperate a situation becomes, the harder it becomes to trust someone and it is here that the particular quality of trustworthiness called loyalty is put to the test. Loyalty is faithfulness at its most personal and its most committed. It says:

"I will be here in the bad times as well as the good."

"I will be for you even when everyone else is against you."

"I will defend you, even at cost or risk to myself."

The heart of covenant is the bond of personal loyalty between the parties, and in his covenant with us God constantly assures us of his loyalty, *"Never will I leave you, never will I forsake you."*[11] Loyalty is thus an essential component of the most important and most intimate of our relationships. We rightly despise the "fair weather friend" or the leader or others who desert commitments because the going gets rough.

At the same time, the clash of loyalties can be the most agonising of moral predicaments, and it is vital that we are clear on the question of priorities. In the Scriptural teaching the claims of covenant take precedence over all other obligations, first in terms of God's covenant with us, and second in the terms of the covenant of marriage.

Reliability – trustworthiness at its most conscientious

To be able to rely on someone means that we can depend on them to do what they have undertaken to do without the need for us to check up on them to see whether it is being done or not. The reliable person is self motivated to keep their undertakings. To them reliability is a matter of conscience.

Reliability and dependability are built up by consistent faithfulness in small things but to those in authority these small things often have a symbolic significance far beyond their immediate importance. In the parable of the talents, when the first servant came and said, *"Sir, your mina has earned ten more,"* the master's reply was, *"Well done, my good servant, because you have been trustworthy in a very small matter, take charge of ten cities."*[12]

On the other hand, if a person is unreliable in small things, the judgment is likely to be, "If you cannot trust him in little things, what will he be like if we strike a real crisis?"

Consistency – trustworthiness at its most principled

To be able to trust someone we need predictable responses on their part. How can you trust someone who today is wildly enthusiastic about a project and tomorrow couldn't care less, or who one day treats something as a great joke and the next day gets furiously angry about it.

Similarly it is difficult to trust the very impulsive person because you are never very sure what he or she will do, whether they will jump to the wrong conclusion without proper consideration, or leap into action on very inadequate information.

Consistency like character requires that we make decisions on the basis of principles and not moods or expediency, and that we act, not on whim or impulse but on the basis of a rational and sensible application of those principles to the facts of the situation.

Keeping promises – faithfulness to our word

Being true to our word means keeping promises or vows even when it is inconvenient or costly to do so. People nowadays make promises very lightly and break them with so little compunction that we have ceased to consider a promise a matter of any great consequence. The modern promise appears to have an unexpressed proviso that says, "Provided it is still convenient or my feelings don't change, or circumstances don't dictate otherwise, I promise..." With such conditional promises, it is no wonder that people's commitment also tends to be conditional. How can you commit yourself unreservedly to someone who may back out of their undertakings if something better turns up?

I have to understand that when I make a promise I am not merely expressing a proposal or an intention:

(a) I am making a serious and earnest commitment as to how I am going to act in the future, and

(b) I intend that commitment to taken and relied on as an assurance that I will, in fact, act the way I have declared, and

(c) I am taking upon myself the duty or obligation to fulfil my pledged word when the time comes, no matter how difficult or costly that may be. In other words, I have limited my freedom of action in that particular situation because I consider myself duty bound to act or do exactly what I said I would.

God's promises are his serious commitments on which we are meant to rely, and in making them God has limited his freedom of action because he has declared in advance what in certain circumstances he will always do.[13] Our promises must be taken just as seriously.

Honesty – faithfulness to the truth

It is very difficult to trust someone when you cannot depend on them to tell the truth or when you suspect that they are deceiving you. *"A truthful witness gives honest testimony, but a false witness tells lies."*[14]

But trust is also made difficult by certain ways of communicating that we sometimes do not recognise as being deceptive, or that give the impression of being deceptive.

1. Telling less than the whole truth; what we say is true but it does not give the whole picture.

2. Speaking indirectly or obliquely so that the person is left trying to guess or infer what we mean, or what we are getting at. It is very difficult to trust a statement that has a hidden agenda or leaves us trying to "read between the lines".

3. Communicating the facts but not our feelings so that the other person is left in the dark about how we really view the matter.

4. Dressing the same message up in different ways for different people. This is a common failing of leaders and it never fails to generate mistrust when the hearers start comparing the different messages.

Trust – crisis or process?

Trust, like its more religious term faith, is both a crisis and a process, it is a point of decision but also something that emerges and develops gradually over time. We need to understand both aspects.

Trust as decision

We can place our trust in a moment of decision. I hire the accountant for a job where she will have major responsibilities, I consent to put myself under the doctor's treatment or I say "Yes" to a marriage proposal. I may have all sorts of questions and doubts in the run up to the decision but there comes a point where I either do it or back off. I know when the die is cast or the commitment is made. To change my mind thereafter or to revert to uncertainty smacks already of disloyalty or breach of trust. The more costly the decision to trust has been, the more seriously will I take my commitment and the more reluctant I will be to change my mind.

This can illuminate the whole understanding of the place of faith in our relationship with God. We begin to see that faith is not some capricious choice or condition that God has laid down as the basis of salvation. *Faith is a necessary condition of any personal relationship.* Built into the moral universe in which we live is the fact that all relationships involve trust. The strangest thing would be to discover that it was possible to relate personally to God in a way that did not have this element of faith or trust. Whatever such a relationship would be, of one thing you can be quite certain, it would not be a personal relationship.

Trust as a process

But trust is also a process, trust has to grow. One act of trust is not enough to provide it with enough strength to survive the rigours of a relationship. That is why the New Testament gives far more attention to the growth and nurture of faith after we

51

have come to Christ than it does to the initial act of faith that puts us into Christ.

This is unquestionably a major lack in much of what is taught on marriage skills. Emphasis is rightly placed on love and understanding but very little on how to build trust or develop trustworthiness. If we gave trust the attention and care it deserves, far fewer marriages would founder on broken promises and unfaithfulness.

Parents too, need to know how to bring their children up to be trustworthy teenagers and dependable adults, and employers need to know how to develop responsibility in their staff.

Here are some guidelines to get you started, firstly to develop our capacity to trust others and at the same time encouraging the growth of trustworthiness in the people we trust, and secondly, to develop our own trustworthiness so that people will more readily trust us.

How to build trust

Building our trust in the other person and building their trustworthiness

1. Remember that you have to take risks, there is no such thing as costless trust. The cost of trust is, as we have seen, the inevitable vulnerability that occurs if we let real outcomes go out of our hands into the hands of another person.

Sometimes we say that trust has to be earned and that is true, but it is also true that I cannot prove that I can be trusted unless someone first takes the risk of trusting me. In the parable of the talents in Luke 19, the servants had the chance to prove their faithfulness only because the nobleman first took the risk of trusting them with his money.

2. In first trusting someone, play to their strengths not their weaknesses, that is, trust them to do things that they are good at doing, things they like doing and things they are sure to succeed at. This is very important with children and new or inexperienced employees, and it also reduces the risk of failure. It is also important that our steps in trusting others should succeed early.

3. Be prompt to praise accomplishment of the assignment and to express your confidence. To be trusted is to be honoured, and to be recognised as trustworthy is a very rewarding experience. *"Well done, good and faithful servant! You have been faithful with a few things; I will put you in charge of many things! Come and share your master's happiness."*[15]

By the same token our capacity to trust grows with confessing our faith – "I can trust you." Here as always, believing and confessing go together.[16]

4. Model faithfulness and trustworthiness in your own character. People, and particularly children, learn by modelling. They will prize trustworthiness as a virtue and seek to emulate it, only when they see it practised consistently by those they look up to and admire most, such as parents, leaders and other role models.

5. Ensure that success is rewarded with greater responsibility, but remember to increase the challenge in small steps. The rule is line upon line, line upon line, a little here, a little there.[17] Be patient, remember you are building trust, not testing its limits, therefore do not stretch your own or the other person's capacity too far too fast.

6. If the person fails, give them another chance. Go back to where they succeeded last time and start again. And **be very cautious about saying, "I trusted you and you let me down."** Trust is such a fragile thread at the beginning that if you tell a person that you don't trust them it will be a long time before they can believe your later assurances that now you do trust them.

7. Distinguish carefully between trusting someone and testing them or trying them out. There is a legitimate place for trying a person out but it is not the same as trusting. If my boss says to me, "I'm trying you out to see if you can do this job" and I fail, all that we have found out is that I am unable to do the job. But if he says, "I am trusting you to do this job" and then I fail, not just my ability but my trustworthiness is in question.

8. Never say to someone, "I trusted you and you let me down," if they didn't know beforehand that they were on trust, and had accepted that responsibility.

Building people's trust in our trustworthiness

Trustworthiness is built in very unspectacular ways, with very little panache and flair, therefore it is more difficult for some temperaments than others, not because it is hard but because it is painstaking. Here is what you need to do:

1. Creat a climate of trustworthiness and dependability, for example:

(a)   Be reliable and conscientious in discharging responsibilities and fulfilling tasks or obligations.

(b)   Be scrupulous in keeping promises even when it is inconvenient and irksome or costly to do so.

(c)   Be consistent, act out of principle not on whim or impulse.

(d)   Be meticulous in keeping confidences, but never promise confidentiality without knowing the details first.

2. Be honest, tell the whole truth not just a part of it, and share your feelings as well as your thoughts. Ensure that you are telling it the way it is and there are no inferences that need to be made or hidden agendas to create suspicion.

3. Work at your character. Remember that a crisis does not create character, it only shows the character that is already there.

(a)   Know yourself and the weaknesses you have to guard against or strengthen.

(b)   Don't allow yourself to take the soft option or the easy way out. The right way is generally the more difficult of the options.

(c)   Never compromise your principles under pressure or for the sake of expediency.

5. Be cheerful and avoid complaining in the bad times or lapsing into self pity when the going gets rough. It is extraordinarily difficult to have confidence in someone who is always sorry for themselves.

Trust and leadership

Trust is a dominant element in the relationship between people and their leaders. People have to trust their leaders, and leaders have to trust their people which is something again. The greater responsibility in the relationship rests on the leaders. Leaders are the ones who decide what is to be done, and when it is to be done and who is to do it. They exercise power. Moreover they generally have access to more information than anybody else, and knowledge is also power. So they have more power than anybody else. Therefore the position of leader is called a *position of trust*.

It is very important to understand this because if the leader fails, in the way he exercises the role of leader or if he fails morally in his private life, a breach of trust is involved. Not many Christian leaders recognise this. The cry is sometimes, "Why should I be treated differently from other people who also have these moral lapses?" As far as the moral failing is concerned, whether it is adultery or lying or financial dishonesty, the plain answer is that they should not be treated differently from anybody else. But something else is involved that is not involved with people not in leadership; there has been a breach of trust. This is a separate issue that has to be addressed. Restoration is not complete until trust is also restored.

When we talk about people trusting their leaders, however, we have to ask what exactly it is that they are trusting? In other words what is the particular area of dependence that is involved when I put my trust in someone as my leader?

Firstly, I am trusting their judgment. I am depending on them to have got the right goals and to have got the goals right. The job of the leader has to do with the future; the "lead" that the leader has, as Robert Greenleaf rightly points out, is that he is better than others at the job of pointing direction, at dealing with a future that hasn't arrived yet. Now I cannot see things as clearly as the leader does. If I could I would be the leader. So I have largely to depend on his judgment and his assessment of the possibilities that lie in the future. That is why it is always harder to trust an untried or inexperienced leader, we have no past record to go on. With an experienced leader, his abilities and his judgment and his capacities are better known; there is something to go on to decide if or how far I am willing to trust him.

Leaders for their part need to be aware of the kind of commitment they are demanding from their people, and the kind of faith step that is involved. Trust as we have seen makes me vulnerable because I have handed over some part of my destiny to somebody else, and if this commitment is a major one, failure on the part of the person I have trusted will bring a good deal of uncertainty and fear into my situation. Fear almost always leads to anger because anger is an emergency emotion, whose purpose is to harden us to face a situation of threat or danger. Since the leader has been the one whose failure has created the threat to my security, it will not be surprising if he also becomes the object of my anger. Breach of trust in leadership always generates a highly charged emotional atmosphere, but anger, if this is involved, is not the totally unfair and undeserved response that leaders sometimes consider it to be.

Secondly, I have put my trust in the leader's *integrity*, that is the leader's honesty and truthfulness. I learned a very important lesson regarding this in the mid 60s when we were involved with the very beginnings of the charismatic renewal amongst Roman Catholics in New Zealand. The dear saints who gathered in those first prayer meetings knew so little, they believed everything I told them. I think for a time they almost looked on me as a kind of unofficial cardinal – very flattering and very dangerous. Then one day I told them something I really thought I had got from God, only to find out during the following week that I had got it totally wrong. I had a couple of sleepless nights I can tell you. I thought "If I tell them what has happened they will never trust me again." But I could not get off the hook, so the very next time we met I faced up to it. I said, "Last week I told you such and such and I thought I really had it from God. The fact of the matter is I made a complete mistake, I was just wrong, I gave you bad advice."

From that point on, I discovered, they really started to trust me. People do not require their leaders to be infallible (sometimes leaders think they have to be infallible) but they do require them to be honest. People will follow a leader almost anywhere provided they are sure that if the leader leads down the wrong path and discovers it he will admit his mistake and lead them back to safe ground. To make a mistake in leading may be costly, but to make a mistake and then try to justify it is fatal. It leaves the leader open to real deception.

Thirdly, I have to trust in the leader's *perseverence*, that is that he will hang in there even when the going gets tough. It is the leader's responsibility to keep the group on track and heading towards the goal even when everybody else is ready to give it away as a bad job. Anybody can lead when things are going well and enthusiasm and hope are cresting. When failure looms as a distinct possibility and the vision is waning is when the real character of a leader emerges. Does she want to be identified only with success? If so she is more concerned with her reputation than with the goal. Is he likely to bale out rather than have his track record tainted with a failure? If those who follow have that uneasy suspicion they will be unlikely to stick with the leader through the bad times.

The criteria for trust thus come down to two things, one is capability and the other is character. Of these character is the more important. Not very many mistakes are fatal. Incompetence in leadership is damaging but if the leader is willing to learn most of that can in time be overcome. Character is more important, flaws there can be fatal. The inability to learn from mistakes is more likely to be because of a character defect than a lack of intelligence. But character does not develop or change suddenly. Crises do not create character, they only bring to light the character that is already there. Trust therefore depends on my knowledge of the person's character as well as my confidence in his ability. His ability may assure me that in a given situation he will know what is the right thing to do, only character will give me confidence that he will in fact do the thing that he knows is right.

Not only do people need to trust their leaders, leaders have to trust their people. My experience is that generally leaders do not do it as well as their people do, which is why it is very often difficult to lead leaders. Leaders do not generally have a great deal of confidence in the people they are leading. Whenever I find in an organisation or church, that leaders have reserved to themselves a final right to decide, or a reserve of power just in case things go wrong, then I suspect that the root of it is that they have only a conditional or restricted trust in their people. They cannot then complain if the trust people have in them is also conditional.

References

1. Romans 4:20–21.
2. Hebrews 11:1.
3. James 2:26.
4. Isaiah 43:19 ASB.
5. Romans 4:3 ASB.
6. 1 Corinthians 4:2.
7. Psalm 27:3.

8. 2 Corinthians 7:4.
9. Proverbs 31:10–11.
10. Psalm 41:9.
11. Hebrews 13:5–6.
12. Luke 19:17.
13. Hebrews 6:13–19.
14. Proverbs 12:17.
15. Matthew 25:21.
16. Romans 10:8–9.
17. Isaiah 28:10 ASB.

Chapter 5

Made for Honour

If the most rugged and the most enduring of the four elements that go to make up a relationship is love, and the most fragile is trust, certainly the most overlooked and neglected in our society today is respect or honour.

Yet the Bible is full of strong imperatives regarding giving honour. We are not so much recommended to do it, as commanded. We are commanded to honour God, first of all and above all; in fact the root of man's sin according to Paul in Romans 1:21 is that knowing God, they did not honour or glorify him as God.

We are also commanded to honour our father and our mother.[1] Obedience to parents belongs to our childhood, honour is binding on us throughout our life. It is part of the moral law and indeed the first commandment that has a promise attached to it. We will see the significance of this later. But we are also to honour our employers, our leaders and the elders of the church; husbands are to respect their wives and wives are to respect their husbands and the married state is to be held in honour by all. Surprisingly we are to honour the less than successful and the disadvantaged – the widows, the elderly and the less gifted members of the body. We are indeed to honour one another and all men regardless of their state. Even more amazing is the fact that honour is not only to be given by us to God, it is given by God to us. Of his people God says, *"Because you are honoured and I love you;"* and again, *"Those who honour me I will honour."*[2] What we have in the Bible is the picture of a society built on the mutual flow of honour and respect, amongst all the members.

59

What is honour or respect?

Honour or respect is the recognition of the other person's worth or value. When I give honour or respect I acknowledge the other's dignity, value and worthiness. Therefore God is to be honoured before all and above all because he is supremely the highest value in the universe, indeed of far more value than the entire universe. But honour also recognises the worth and value of men and women made in the image of God. This honouring is crucial for a number of reasons.

Firstly, when I recognise the value of people I become aware of how incredibly rich my life is because it is surrounded and interpenetrated by so many worthy and valuable men and women. My life acquires thereby a sense of meaning and significance. If I do not give respect or honour, or worse if I dishonour the people around me, I impoverish my own life, I demean its significance because I act as if it relates to worthless people.

Secondly, it is only when I am myself receiving honour and respect from others that I can feel worthy or worthwhile in myself. There is undoubtedly a direct correlation between the great numbers of people in our society with a low or poor self-image and the way in which, as a society, we major on dishonouring. We dishonour God and his word, we heap disrespect on the institutions of our society, we scorn the past, moral values, parenthood, authority and the rights of others. Disrespect and dishonour is not so much flaunted as glorified. Many people in the media make a living out of it. Everything is to be shown up as flawed and sham. We then reap what we have sown, as the Psalmist points out:

> *"The wicked freely strut about,*
> *When what is vile is honoured among men."*[3]

But we also reap the result in ourselves. We are dishonoured, we suffer in self-esteem and self-respect, we are smitten with a sense of worthlessness.

Finally, trying to give ourselves a good self-image is a no-way street. It cannot be done, I cannot give myself honour, in spite of what all the books on self-psychology tell us. We are dependent on one another, our self-image is formed out of our relationships. A poor self-image may be evidenced by an inability to form or sustain good relationships with other people, but in the first place it is formed by bad relationships or lack of good relationships and the lack is chiefly a lack of affirmation or honour.

Measures of value

If respect or honour is the recognition of worth or value we have to decide where value comes from or how it arises. All value is imputed. The worth of anything is simply the valuation people place on it. I may spend $1 million designing and producing a super widget, and a similar sum marketing it, but if nobody will buy a super widget its value is zero or at most the scrap value of the materials. On the other hand people may pay a fortune for a rare stamp whose value in terms of materials, two square centimetres of paper, is zero. The things people respect or honour therefore reveal very clearly the values on which a society or community is built. They give us a basis for comparing our society with others or our own society today with what it was in other eras. Clearly western society places the highest value on entertainment, sporting ability and material wealth since it is those who succeed in these areas who receive most honour.

But is this a true value system on which to base our estimate of human beings? If not, what is the value system that ought to be used? **The biblical value system for assessing the worth of men and women has three measures of value to which we now turn**.

Intrinsic value

Instrinsic value is the value that belongs to the essence of a person or thing. For example if you have a gold ornament, you can smash it with a hammer, you can grind it to powder, you can burn it in the fire, but there is a certain value that will survive all these destructive forces – the value of the gold metal. That is its intrinsic value, it is irreducible, inalienable, and indestructible.

My *intrinsic worth* is my value as a person, quite apart from my gifts, my possessions or my accomplishments. **This eternal worth and significance is given to me by God, that is, it also is imputed**. Nothing I can do can add to that and nothing I can do can detract from it. Just as God unconditionally gives me love, so he unconditionally gives me significance. I can still remember the time that dawned on me. Now I realise that if from here on out I am the most brilliant and successful person who ever lived, it will not add one iota to my intrinsic worth. That value is given, not earned or deserved. But if from here on out I fail at everything I do, if I lose my reputation, my health, my possessions, my friends, my ministry or my sanity, none of these endanger my eternal, intrinsic worth one iota. The realisation of this brought a security into my life like few other truths.

The first value that needs to be established in children is this sense of intrinsic worth, when they realise that they are valuable for themselves and for no other reason. They are not on any performance standard to earn it, or maintain it, they have this value and significance in their own right. The realisation of being intrinsically valuable is critical for a child's sense of security and self-worth.

The importance of respecting a person's intrinsic worth cannot be overstressed. The most inept, the most degraded, the most incapable or the most handicapped person alive still has intrinsic worth and value as a person. It is not that the person has value *for* society or for any other end, the person has value as an end in themselves and that value is always to be respected. They have a dignity that belongs to their personhood as eternal beings made in God's image, fallen indeed but redeemed and capable of eternal fellowship with God. Lack of this basic understanding lies behind much of the injustice and oppression in the world today, including abortion, poverty, racial discrimination, prostitution and pornography.

This kind of respect-for-persons however requires us to make a very clear distinction between who a person is and what a person does. Jesus always made that distinction, one of the most remarkable examples being his encounter with the Samaritan woman recorded in John chapter 4. When Jesus said to her, "You have been married five times (in all likelihood she had been divorced rather than widowed), and you are living in a de facto relationship right now," she didn't blow up in his face, or get offended, or say "None of your business." She said *"Sir, I perceive you are a prophet."*[4] That is amazing. I believe it was because by then she really knew that Jesus valued her as a person.

He addressed her in exactly the same terms as he used when speaking to his own mother at the wedding in Cana yet he knew her lifestyle only too well. Because Jesus cared deeply for her he had to face her with her moral failure, yet because she was secure in his acceptance of her as a person she did not feel rejected by the confrontation. It is as though the two of them are standing side by side looking at her life and Jesus says, "It's a mess" and she says, "Yes Lord, it's a terrible mess."

That kind of respect lies at the heart of all redemptive relationships, but you cannot pretend it, and get away with it. People are very sensitive to attitudes. But if it really is there in your heart I discover that you can be as straight and as blunt as need be about the person's lifestyle and they will not feel rejected. They may dispute your evaluation, they may argue their case, but they will not be personally distanced by the fact that you see things differently. But if this respect is not there and in our mind we lump the person and his lifestyle together we face problems. One is that in passing judgment on the lifestyle we also reject the person. The second is that in wanting to accept the person we don't know what to do about the lifestyle. We have no answer to the person who says, "You have to accept me the way I am and that includes my homosexual behaviour or my drug addiction or my dishonesty. Don't dare criticise them or you're judging and Christians are not supposed to judge."

The skill of managing people in the workplace or in the church depends on the same basic distinction. I may have to say, "As a person I totally and unreservedly accept you. As a brother or sister in Christ I accept you unconditionally. But I cannot, and I will not accept your level of performance; something has to be done about that."

The value due to character

The second measure of worth that must be recognised is the value that is due to character. *"A good name is more to be desired than great riches,"* says Proverbs.[5] *"Your name,"* sings the bride to her lover in the Song of Songs, *"is like purified oil."*[6] Names in the Bible always means identity or character. The respect or honour that is due to character is one that badly needs restoring to the value system of our society.

In society today, intellectual capacity, sporting ability, artistic talent, business or political acumen, and personal charisma all rate well above character, and are sometimes considered to excuse or justify the absence of moral standards. Even the church has succumbed to the standards of society to the extent that gift and ministry are honoured more than godly character.

In the New Testament the emphasis is not on gifts, or abilities or talent but on character. Character, rather than charisma is the acid test. For example there is very little clearly laid down as to what an elder does or what the function is of a deacon but there is a lot of attention paid to the kind of men they ought to be. The reason for this is that their role is chiefly governmental, that is they are to establish and to model the standards of Christian life that apply in the Christian community. Not many elderships understand this responsibility. I was called one time to a church plagued with problems of strife and bitterness year after year. They had been through traumas with pastors, with leaders, with senior members of the congregation. When we discussed their true role as elders we came across the real root of the problem. All along those men had lacked the courage to deal effectively with the situation because they had personal problems in the very same area. It was enough to silence their tongue and inhibit their authority. When that was dealt with honestly before the Lord they called the church together, confessed their failure to lead the church aright and established clearly the biblical standard of harmony and acceptance that God lays down for his people. The problems ceased almost immediately.

When I think of character I often think of my father. He was a working man, a labourer all his life, quite unknown outside the small circle of his family and the local Baptist church he attended. Yet when he died he left behind four children all of whom were Christians and all of whom established Christian marriages. He went to his God with about as many faults in his life as there were weeds in his garden, and gardening was his great love. I sometimes wonder what else of lasting value a man can do with his life.

But character will have value for the next generation only if they see it valued by the present generation. If we model an attitude that values personality above character, or success above character, or possessions above character let us not be surprised if our children follow our models.

The value due to performance

There is a third measure of worth and value and that is the recognition given to performance or achievement. Elders who labour hard at preaching and teaching are worthy of double honour, says Paul. We are to render honour in this dimension to those to whom honour is due.[7] In everything we do we ought to have excellence as our goal. We ought to want to be the very best we can be at everything we take on. True we may have limited capacities and giftedness and few of us will ever be worldbeaters even at our best but we can all, like Paul, strive mightily according to the grace of God that is in us. We need to commit ourselves to grow. A little child grows without even trying. Feed her, give her sleep and exercise and loving care and she will grow, but only up to a certain point, only up to a certain natural level of development. That little girl will never grow to become a doctor or a politician or a teacher or a musician unless somewhere along the line she makes a conscious commitment to grow. Our churches are full of "mature Christians". They are Christians who grew up to the natural level of spiritual development about 20 years ago and have hardly changed since then.

It actually does not take herculean efforts or quantum leaps for us to make substantial and observable progress. The leading corporations in the United States, the pace-setters and the blue chip companies do not do any single thing twice as well as anybody else, they just do everything one percent better than anybody else. Excellence, or the way to it, is with this approach, within the reach of every church, every business, every family and every person in every form of relationship. It just means improving our performance marginally in a whole lot of areas. What would happen in a church where over the course of one year every member committed themselves to become just one percent more loving at home, one percent more diligent in their job, and a similar margin more consistent in their Bible study, more caring towards their neighbours, more generous in their giving, more active in community affairs and more sensitive to the voice of God? Within months you would be in the middle of a revival.

How do we place the proper valuation on excellence? By recognising and affirming effort, by rewarding intention as well as result, and by noticing and praising accomplishment. One of my sons was a schoolteacher. He tells me one of his best memories of those sometimes difficult years is that of a Maori colleague who never once came into his classroom without finding something to admire or something to praise, whether it was a poster or a work scheme or a display of some sort. That did more for Mark's commitment to his profession and his desire to do the best job possible than any grading marks or promotions or salary increases.

In everything we need to have a commitment to excellence, doing it with all our heart as for the Lord, rather than for men.[8] God is concerned with results and with performance. *"I the Lord search the heart, I test the mind, even to give to each man according to his ways, according to the results of his deeds."*[9] God gives the power to make wealth. Wealth is not money, money we leave behind, wealth we take with us. Wealth is the skill, expertise and knowledge we acquire in this life by using productively the gifts God has given us.

Applying the measures of value

In giving honour we must be clear as to the measure of value we are using, and the person receiving honour must understand the grounds also.

Measure of value	*How value acquired*	*Honour recognises:*
Intrinsic	Given, not earned	the person's eternal value.
Character	Earned, not given	what the person is or has become.
Performance	Earned, not given	what the person has done or achieved.

A person may achieve outstanding results in a particular field, the arts, sports or business, and yet display a very faulty character. In rightly honouring their achievements we are not automatically approving or respecting their character, nor are we saying that as far as intrinsic worth is concerned they are more valuable than anyone else. By the same token, the fact that a person's character is worthy of respect does not entitle them to be honoured for performance that is mediocre or even inept. Nor can a person's need to have their instrinsic worth and value affirmed be met by praising poor performance or accepting uncritically their character, lifestyle or habitual patterns of behaviour.

The content of honour

As with the other elements of relationships we need to expand our understanding of what we mean by honour or respect because the concept is so neglected in our society that the very words have an old fashioned and outmoded ring about them. Here are some associated terms that will help to enrich the concept of honour. We hunger to be on the receiving end of all of these.

1. Acceptance

The way we use the word acceptance can be a very passive one, even fatalistic "There's nothing you can do about it, you had better just accept it." That is not what we mean by acceptance. Acceptance is the active attitude of receiving that welcomes a person with a genuine warmth and regard. It says in effect, "You are a valuable addition to this group," or "I'm glad you are a part of this church, or family or team." That is what Paul had in mind when he said, *"Accept one another, then, just as Christ accepted you, in order to bring praise to God."*[10]

2. Recognition

Recognition is responding to a person in a way that shows that they have captured our attention as someone unique and individual, and that we are interested in their activities or achievements or opinions. It indicates that we have passed judgment on their quality and have come up with a positive or favourable assessment.

3. Affirmation

Affirmation is strengthening the person's sense of self-worth by drawing attention to their strengths and gifts. Affirmation rests on the truth that all of us were created by God to be good at some things but not good at everything and focuses on what we do well, not what we do poorly. It is catching people out at succeeding. It says, "I think you are marvellous and I would like you to feel that way about yourself." We are so far from understanding honour that statements like this fall strangely on our Christian ears, either in making or receiving them.

4. Appreciation
Appreciation is more subjective than affirmation. It expresses the pleasure we feel in the other person's company or presence, in the way they dress, or the things they talk about or the stimulus of their personality. It says, "I greatly enjoy seeing you the way you are and doing the things you do."

5. Approval
Approval expresses our agreement with and commendation of, a person's performance or actions or opinions. We side with them and express our support for them, and in so doing indicate that we consider their behaviour worthy and worthwhile. Approval says, "I totally agree with what you are doing and in similar circumstances I would do exactly the same."

6. Admiration
This is expressing commendation and praise for a person's achievements or character, but goes further than approval. Approval says, "I would have done exactly the same as you have done;" admiration says, "I couldn't have done it half as well as you have done," or "You set a standard in this that makes me want to emulate you."

7. Acknowledgement
This is giving a person recognition, praise or commendation in public or before other people. In its simplest form it may be in the way we introduce a friend to a group. If I say something like, "It is a real pleasure for me to introduce my very good friend Bill Fauld," it indicates that Bill is a worthy person who stands high in my estimation, and I want the others to behave towards him accordingly.

Showing respect, giving honour

It is not enough to understand the nature of honour or respect, or even to appreciate its importance, we need to know how to convey it. Honour has to be "given" before the other person can receive it; we talk about "paying" our respects. Behind these expressions there is a true sense that merely thinking respectfully about someone or just feeling how worthy or valuable they are, is inadequate unless it is communicated.

Conveying honour verbally

The simplest way to convey honour is to express it in words, simple, sincere statements that convey our affirmation, appreciation, or esteem. We can say it face to face, in which case the person can catch the warmth in our voice and the expression on our face, furthermore we can amplify our meaning in a variety of ways. Or we can do it in writing which may lack the personal impact to some extent but it is more deliberate and intentional and gives a permanent record that the person can read over and over.

Another way in which we convey honour is by speaking well of one another to third parties. Paul did it constantly and his letters to the churches are often full of warm personal commendation of fellow workers or colleagues.[11]

Expressions of praise, esteem, appreciation, affirmation, approval and commendation are all ways of showing honour. Parents need to remember this. Children are born with just two basic needs, the need for love and the need for significance, or the need to feel good about themselves. This latter need has to do with honour and it is not the same as the need for love. True, the child who is loved has a better chance of also feeling honoured, but not necessarily, and certainly the child who is not loved loses on both scores. When honour is lacking a child will suffer even if love is sufficient. The commonest consequence is an inferiority complex or even worse the lack of hope, the lack of the very courage to be. The critical role in this is the father's. Fathering is giving the child his sense of identity and his sense of self-worth. It is instructive to read about the fathering Jesus received. It gave him his identity, *"You are my Son whom I love; with you I am well pleased"* and honour *"That all may honour the Son just as they honour the Father."*[12]

I once took part in a television panel on the problems of parents and children. Before we went on camera I was talking to one of the other panellists, a professor of child development psychology in one of our universities, about the need for models of fathering. I said I wished that I had known the Fatherhood of God in the way I know it now, when my children were young, I would have been a much better father to them than I was. His reply was illuminating. He didn't understand all the fuss about fathering, he said, what the child needed was good parenting and it didn't matter whether it came from a father or a mother. Now I know that the increasing number of one-parent families mean the roles of father and mother have somehow to be filled by the same person, but that is not the divine norm. Fathering and mothering are not the same thing. If I was making a distinction I would say that mothering primarily meets the child's love needs and fathering meets the child's worth needs. They are obviously not watertight compartments, fathers have also to nurture, and mothers have to affirm, but notice your small child – if she falls over and skins her knees it is generally mother she runs to for comfort, but if she comes home from school with something she is quite proud of making it is generally father she wants to show it to. Above all we have to affirm the child's *intrinsic worth*. It is easier for the pretty girl or the bright or athletic boy to be affirmed but what about those who are not beautiful and not all that bright? How do they get their sense of worth? You need to say to your children many times, not only "I love you" but "I think you're great. I'm so proud of you."

Honouring by our behaviour
In addition to explicit expressions of respect or honour we also show it implicitly, but nevertheless clearly, by the way we behave towards one another in certain situations.

1. We convey honour by acknowledging one another in company and supporting each other in public. For example, when we are introduced by name to a group of people and welcomed by them we sense that our significance and worth is somehow being recognised. What we feel is that we are honoured.

2. We show a person honour when we seek their advice, or opinion on a matter of concern to us, or submit our views or proposals for their evaluation and critique and then we treat their advice or opinions seriously. We thereby show that we value their judgment and at least by implication we indicate that we also respect and value them.

3. We honour a person when we have a genuine care and concern for their welfare and their best interests. Such care says to the person that they are valuable and worthwhile and that we desire the best for them even at cost to ourselves.

In the 1960s I was in Australia recruiting tradesmen for companies in New Zealand in the heady days of full employment in our country. We were in Adelaide, interviewing carpenters and an English couple in their early 40s came to see me. We talked about the job and his background and experience and it was obvious he was both suitable and keen to go. His problem was that they had already emigrated once, from England to Australia, and he was unsure about uprooting his wife a second time from her home and friends and starting all over once again. I always remember his wife's response. Even after all these years it sticks in my mind. She turned to him and said "Never mind about me, my dear, it is your career that is important." I remember thinking at the time, "I hope that carpenter appreciates the kind of wife he has." That was respect truly expressed.

4. Respecting or honouring people also means acknowledging their right to:
(a)   Make decisions we would not make,
(b)   Make mistakes we would not make,
(c)   Hold views or opinions we do not hold, and
(d)   Follow the dictates of their own conscience.

This is very important for the attitude of Christians towards one another, and for parents as their children reach adulthood.

5. We show that we honour and respect people when we insist on treating them as responsible persons who can take charge of their own lives. Therefore we will confront them when they are performing well below their capacity or when there are things that are wrong or dangerous in their lives. In so doing we are saying that we consider them too valuable to allow them to spoil their lives or their testimony by not dealing with the problems, and we are prepared to risk offending them by speaking out.

6. Giving gifts can express not only our love, but also honour. The gift is seen as a token, or symbol of the regard we have for one another and the worth we see in one another. That is why offerings are part of our worship to God; *"Honour the Lord with your wealth, with the firstfruits of all your crops."*[13]

7. We honour one another by giving ourselves to each other in relationships. For example in offering a person our friendship we are also expressing our sense of their value and worthiness compared with other people because we want them to have a special place in our life and affections, and ourselves to have a similar place in theirs. That is why there is something important about honour at the heart of sexual union in marriage. It is enshrined in the words of the marriage ceremony, "With my body I thee honour." It is perhaps the greatest honour a man can give a woman or a woman can give a man. Therefore divine wisdom reserved it for the covenant of marriage. It sums up all the categories that have gone before, the words, the looks, the touch, the being present for one another, and the care for the other's needs and interests. Today in the media, marital fidelity is consistently and characteristically lampooned, yet any minister, any priest or any counsellor who has had to deal with a person going through the trauma of discovering their marriage partner has been unfaithful, will tell you the same thing. Deeper than any feelings of anger or hurt or jealousy is the sense of having been dishonoured, of being robbed of dignity and personal significance. It is an issue that is rarely addressed adequately and because it is not dealt with properly, many a sincerely attempted reconciliation comes to ruin.

Non-verbal ways of showing honour

We communicate in two main ways, one is verbal, that is in words, and the other is non-verbal, that is in gestures, expressions, body language, the pitch and tone of our voice and so on. Sometimes the message we communicate in words is different from the message we communicate by these latter means. Communication experts tell us that the non-verbal message is at least five times more effective than the verbal message and if the two messages conflict the receiver will always believe the non-verbal communication. We say, "You could tell by the way she said it she was just being sarcastic."

Here are some of the non-verbal ways in which honour is communicated. We need to pay careful attention to them because often we are not very aware of non-verbal messages we are sending and are often taken by surprise when we discover how people react.

1. By touch, for example a handshake, a slap on the shoulder or a kiss on the cheek, a hug when you meet, even when your children are grown up, or the spontaneous, for-no-reason-at-all touches between husband and wife communicate not only affection but honour. That is why, when an offered handshake is ignored, it is felt to be insulting or dishonouring.

Men, and women, in the workplace and the rough and tumble of competitive business activity are continually in situations that can erode or deal blows to their self-confidence and self-respect. Being passed over for promotion, losing a sale, making a mistake and being reprimanded by the supervisor, being in a job where you have to take orders from somebody else all the time as though you were incapable of making decisions, getting into financial difficulties, being sacked or being made redundant, all render us highly vulnerable to self-doubt. So do aging, ill health, and the gradual abandonment of long cherished dreams as clearly unattainable. In these circumstances a husband and a wife can shore up and reinforce each other's damaged self-confidence better than anybody else on earth – or they can devastate it more thoroughly because they know only too well each other's weaknesses and vulnerabilities.

2. By the way we look at one another. This is behind the use of the word "regard" in English to mean both "to view" and "to respect", and why "looking up" to somebody is honouring them, while "looking down" on them is holding them in contempt.

The two things we cannot control with our will are the tone of our voice and the look in our eyes. If we despise someone, it will show in our eyes, if we dislike them, our eyes are a dead giveaway. If we love or admire or respect someone, it will also affect the way we look at them. Jesus said, *"Your eye is the lamp of your body"*[14] therefore what is in our minds and in our hearts will inevitably show in our eyes.

Watch a little toddler absorbed in his play in the middle of the room, then becoming aware of the loving, smiling, proud looks of parents and family. You can see him start to glow inside. What is happening? His little spirit is absorbing honour. Scientists tell us that a baby gets its first sense of significance long before it can understand words. Where does it get it from? From its mother's face. From that loving smiling face a baby gets the sense of its worth and value. But if the mother's face is not smiling, or is absent, a baby can get a feeling of unconditional badness, of utter worthlessness. You had better believe that. I have spoken to adults who all their lives have felt a nothing, have felt that only bad things ought to happen to them, and such is the power of a self-image that it produced in and for them the very things they expected.

Now I begin to understand why the old men and women of the Bible were always wanting to see God's face. *"Do not hide your face from me,"* cries David *"Let me see your face."*[15] Where does our ultimate sense of worth and significance come from? From God's face. When it is hidden from us we are derelict of any inner sense of significance.

3. By giving a person a special place of honour. This may be a formal recognition of the honour due to a position, the throne of a ruler or the bench of a judge, or as informal as a seat at the head of the table at a meal, a place next to the chairman at a meeting, or a seat on the platform at a public gathering. It may also be stepping aside and allowing a person to go ahead of us through a door or precede us into a gathering. The spatial concept of honour also comes into the language of respect. We say of a person whom we hold in high regard, "She has a special place in our estimation."

4. By "being present" for a person, that is to say, being aware of and attentive to them, and to whatever they are saying or doing. Often when we are physically present our mind or our attention is elsewhere. Children are very sensitive to this. Remember the time when your small child was telling you something and you kept the conversation going with occasional Yes's, I see's and Is that so's while you figured out the shopping list or what was wrong with the motor mower. There was that indignant yell, "You're not *listening!*" Being present for the other person is active attention to what is being said; it is also being present even when there is no actual spoken conversation. You begin to talk to someone at a party and half way through the second sentence you become aware that they are looking over your left shoulder at a point on the other side of the room. What does it feel like? You feel dishonoured, insignificant, put down.

I remember one of our little granddaughters who stayed with us one summer. Our house is right on the seashore and we were down on the beach building a sandcastle. Little Lydia would have been about six at the time. All of a sudden she looked up at me and said "Grandad, why are you giving me so much of your time?" It was a modest enough investment of time but what was happening? The little lass was feeling important, valued and significant because somebody was giving her time.

There are few things that will enrich the quality of our relationships more than the recovery and reintroduction of mutual honour and respect. A person who is honoured and knows it, has thereby a great stake in behaving honourably. A person who is persistently dishonoured eventually sees no point in doing anything else but living down to the level of people's expectation of him or her.

Humanity was made for honour. When God first made man and woman they were "crowned with glory and honour." We need to bring back mutual respect and honour at every level of our society, between husbands and wives, parents and children, teachers and pupils, workers and management, pastors and people. It begins with honouring God, and discovering the amazing truth about God's attitude towards us *"Since you are precious and honoured in my sight and because I love you . . ."*[16]

References

1. Ephesians 6:2.
2. Isaiah 43:4; 1 Samuel 2:30.
3. Psalm 12:8.
4. John 4:19.
5. Proverbs 22:1.
6. Song of Songs 1:3.
7. 1 Timothy 5:17; Romans 13:7.
8. Colossians 3:24.
9. Jeremiah 17:10 ASB.
10. Romans 15:7.

11. Romans 16:1; 1 Corinthians 16:15–18; 2 Corinthians 8:23–24.
12. Mark 1:11; John 5:23.
13. Proverbs 3:9.
14. Matthew 6:22.
15. Psalm 27:9.
16. Isaiah 43:4.

Chapter 6

Understanding Understanding

From our earliest years we have a longing to make ourselves understood. Disappointed as children we wail "You don't understand." As adults we complain "I can't get him to understand," or "I'll never understand her." Worse still is the feeling of being somehow alienated and shut out of the world of humankind, "Nobody understands me." One of our most basic needs is to be understood. We do not expect other people to agree with us; nor are we necessarily looking for confirmation or congratulation. These are gratifying for sure but we can manage without them just so long as we feel that somebody understands us, somebody knows what we are feeling and somebody appreciates our real desires and intentions. No one can long survive without that.

When we do find someone who genuinely wants to understand us, the remarkable thing is that we feel immediately released from the need to justify our behaviour or opinions. A channel is opened for us to communicate in a way that makes comprehension possible. Where once we were tongue tied and confused, words and ideas emerge with clarity and profusion. The relief is enormous. Amongst all the ears into which we could speak we have found one that is truly open to hear. It is a pearl of great price, and we will do almost anything to maintain and cultivate that relationship.

The fact that the experience of being understood is both a relief and a rarity draws attention to a strange feature. Although the need to be understood is such a powerful factor and causes us to seek out relationships with people, it is not matched by an equal hunger on our part to know others. We simply do not have the same eager longing to know as we have to be known.

St Francis of Assisi was doubtless aware of that when he prayed "Let me not seek to be understood but to understand." There are probably two main reasons for this kind of bias. One is our incurable self-centredness. Truth to tell we consider ourselves much more interesting than other people, our problems more important, our opinions more compelling. The other is our intuitive, and correct, realisation that to really understand another person is going to take a long time. You do not understand the complexities and depths in a person in one dazzling flash of insight. Results come by a process of slow accretion, little hints, half observed cues, tentative assessments. But our modern society built on instant results leaves us ill equipped for such long voyages of discovery. If the answer is not forthcoming by next Friday, or the following Tuesday at the latest we decide it is probably not worth the effort. That is why many people today settle for superficial contacts and temporary, uncommitted relationships and all the time wonder why they are so dissatisfied and lonely even amongst "friends".

The beginning and the end

We deal with understanding as the last of the four elements of relationships because in a sense it is the goal towards which all the others lead and the end they all serve. Knowledge of each other is the purpose or aim of relationships, *"Then shall I know fully, just as I also have been fully known."*[1] That is the drive within us towards being known. The other drive is the sin-induced withdrawal from relationships *"I heard the sound of thee in the garden and I was afraid because I was naked so I hid myself."*[2] We are torn between the fear that makes us want to hide from each other and the created longing to be known by each other.

But understanding or knowledge is also the prerequisite for the other elements to develop. I cannot love somebody I do not really know. I may be loving an image or an idea that has no correspondence with reality. "She's not the girl I fell in love with." "I fell in love with a fantasy, the reality has been a terrible shock." We have heard dozens of variations on this theme. I cannot trust somebody I do not know or cannot understand. That would be blind faith at its most reckless and presumptuous. *"The sheep simply will not follow a stranger but will flee from him because they do not know the voice of strangers."*[3] And it is as difficult to respect or honour someone I do not know as it is to impute the correct value to an unknown quantity.

The truth is that you cannot lead people, you cannot serve people and you cannot manage people unless, to some considerable extent, you take the trouble to know them and to understand them. Otherwise the best grasp of management principles and a mastery of all the theories of industrial or interpersonal psychology turn out to be of little help in dealing with John Smith because John Smith does not live by the principles in a textbook any more than you do. He lives out of the mysterious and profound complexities of motivation that make him a unique individual. Unless I learn to know and respect that unique individual I am fumbling in the dark in all my dealings with him. There are, in fact, no measurable inputs that can be relied upon to yield predictable results without having regard to the unpredictable elements within the individual person.

Why do we want to be understood?

At one time I think I looked on relationships as somehow peripheral in my life. They belonged at the circumference where the circle of my life touched the circle of other people's lives. In political terms they belonged to the ministry of external affairs. **Now I realise that relationships are at the very centre of our being, they are of the very essence of our personhood**. The two most fundamental statements ever made about man are in the first two chapters of Genesis, the first is that man is made in the image of God; the second is that it is not good for man to be alone.[4] There we have the essential elements of humanity encapsulated.

Firstly we need to understand what it means when we read that man is made in the image of God. Image ought to be read as a verb, not a noun. Man is a God-imager. He is created to image and reflect, in human terms, the life and nature of God. But God is a God of relationships, a Trinity, an eternal society of Father, Son and Holy Spirit, one God. Therefore man or woman can never be treated as an individual in isolation, but always as a person-in-relationship.

Secondly we need to take with full seriousness, God's statement that it is not good for the human creature to be alone. Only relationship, face to face, heart to heart, person to person with our own kind, can end that alone-ness.

But it goes deeper than merely having company alongside us to overcome our solitariness. I need other people in order to know myself. Because I am always man-in-relationship I cannot even know myself in isolation. Self-knowledge is an inner experience but it is never found by looking in, it does not come by introspection. I truly know myself only as I act and interact within relationships. It is when I am seeking to know and understand the other person that I discover most clearly who I am myself. And it is often only when I am struggling to make myself understood to the other person that I begin to discern the patterns in my own psyche or the elements in my motivation are discerned and the disjointed pieces knit together, so that I suddenly cry "Now I can see what I have been trying to do ... "

Of course I do not always get my self-understanding right. The ability of the human heart to rationalise or otherwise deceive itself is well documented both in Scripture and experience. But it is often only when my grandiose self-deceptions are brought out and paraded for another's inspection that their falsity is shown up. When I have only myself against which to measure my self-estimates, the possibility of error and delusion escalates. Fears, complexes, inhibitions and self-doubts also flourish in the dark. Bringing them out into the open and sharing them with even one other person has a salutary effect, sometimes humbling, very often liberating, but always tending towards realism.

There is something more that I learned only recently. Often when we have been given what seems to us a profound insight, or we have been through some deep experience, there is a sad sense of something that is going to be lost, something that will die with us because there is no-one with whom we can share it. You feel that if even one person was to hear they would somehow be preserved, they would not be lost to human memory. I am eternally grateful that for me at one time there was someone who was willing to be the repository of my confidence, but now I grieve for all the other treasures of the human heart and spirit that are lost because there were no ears to hear them. Those who are gifted to communicate can pass on to others what they have conceived but brilliance of communication and brilliance of spirit do not often go together. Today we have a surfeit of brilliant communication with flawless techniques, but often the content is banal or worse. Yet breathtakingly beautiful insights and profound collisions with truth come to ordinary people, but they do not add to the human deposit because we have not the time or discernment to encourage the treasure out of the earthen vessels. I know something of what is there because in 25 years or more of counselling people I am aware that my life has been permanently and continuously enriched by what they have shared of their hearts with me.

How do we know each other?

The great fascination and the great enchantment of all relationships surely lies in probing the mystery of being, the discovery of the real person to whom I relate who is inside that body, looking at me through those eyes, and back of that behaviour. Indeed so great is the mystery that some have concluded that real knowledge of one another and real communication from person to person is impossible. All I really know, in this view, is what I experience of my own outer and inner worlds. All I can send to, or receive from another person are partial, imperfect, coded reports of each other's experience. I have no way of knowing whether these messages carry the same significance to the one who receives them as the meaning I intend, or whether the interpretation I place on the other's message to me is in fact what they meant to communicate.

As against this, the Bible insists that real communication is possible, not yet perfect or complete, but real; knowledge of persons is possible, not yet perfect but real and meaningful. That is because communication and personal knowledge both existed before man was created, having been from all eternity within the being of God. When God created the animals, we read in Genesis 1 that God blessed them and said, *"Be fruitful and increase in number..."*; but when God created mankind God blessed them, and God *said to them "Be fruitful and increase in number..."* [5] With Adam and Eve dialogue is possible, a message can be heard and understood and replied to. Therefore we find that not only does God know man, but man knows God, and man also knows woman, *"This is bone of my bone and flesh of my flesh..."* [6]

In spite of this, the way in which we know and understand another person is by no means self-evident. If it were it would not pose so many difficulties or require the literature on the subject that is published every year. So often the "how to" eludes us. What is the difference between knowing about a person and knowing the person? There is obviously something more involved than just a face to face encounter. You can work with somebody for years, you may see that person and talk with them regularly yet say in the end "I never really got to know her," or "I never felt I knew the real person." On the other hand you can meet someone just once, or merely correspond with somebody, or rarely still, read something he or she has written and out of that alone have a very clear glimpse of the essential person that is there. What makes the difference?

The role of the human spirit

The essential thing to understand is that we "know" a person with our spirit. When it comes to knowing a person, it is our human spirit that does the knowing. Knowledge of persons is essentially spiritual knowledge, *"For who among man knows the thoughts of a man except the man's spirit within him. In the same way no one knows the thoughts of God except the Spirit of God"* (1 Corinthians 2:11).

In personal encounter we relate to the other, spirit to spirit. If there is no contact at this level there is no personal understanding and no personal knowing. Think of the occasions when you spoke to somebody and you knew that you had "clicked". The vibes were right, or you were "on the same wavelength" or however you express it. What did you feel like afterwards? You felt alive, excited, exhilarated, sometimes euphoric. What has happened is that you have touched spirit. Even when the reaction is not so dramatic you still know that it is real; it may be wordless, to outsiders it may be eventless or undiscernible, but you know that there has been real contact, heart communion, the flow of life between you. Contrast those experiences with the times when an invisible glass wall has been between you and the other person. You exchange words, platitudes, arguments, information, criticisms. How do you feel afterwards? Bored, frustrated, drained, disappointed, dis-spirited? You have reached out for spirit and struck a barrier, hit an impenetrable shield.

This is the real heart of the matter, scarcely ever dealt with satisfactorily in books on communication. Communication between persons and knowledge of persons is at the level of the human spirit. The mind at this level is incapable on its own of doing the job. Nor is it just a matter of being in touch with our feelings and letting our feelings hang out. Feelings or emotions are a result or a by-product. The real person is behind the feelings and behind the thoughts, and truly accessible only as we reach his or her human spirit.

Words, the vehicle of the spirit

The question then is, how do we make that bridge between spirit and spirit? Can we do it deliberately or does it just happen? It happens but we can learn how to do it, better and more often. We do it often through words. Words are the vehicle of spirit. Jesus said in John 6:63 *"The words that I have spoken to you are spirit, and they are life."* As Ellul has finely pointed out, language is the most distinctively human thing about us. Something occurs in the inaccessible interior of another person, but when these things are communicated in words and I hear and understand them, there is produced within me a correspondence with what is within the other person. That is the wonder of the Word of God. That which takes place within the inaccessible interior of God, is uttered, the word comes forth from the Father's bosom and when I receive it I can know within my spirit a revelation of the heart of God.

Of course words do not always communicate spirit, they may be trivia, meaningless sounds; they may transmit sterile data; they may be untrue or deceptive. But when they are in spirit and in truth they can communicate the essence of the life of the person. Once I was speaking with a woman whose daughter's marriage was in real trouble. The mother said, "Their problem is that all the time they have known each other they have never been apart. I did most of my courting by letter because David was away at the war. But I discovered things about him and learned to know him better from his letters than I ever would have done otherwise." When she said that I realised that in the Bible, God's fantastic letters about himself, we have in all likelihood, a fuller and clearer revelation of God than if he sat down and talked with us face to face. In the Scriptures we touch his Spirit, revelation is Spirit to spirit.

But for real communication to take place, in the terms we are speaking of, the person has to be "in" the words he says, the singer has to be "in" her song. That means that we must learn to live out of, and speak out of our spirit. It means that we abandon hidden agendas in our speaking; we cease to communicate by inference or speak obliquely in order to give a certain impression or create a certain effect. We learn to speak the truth from the heart. One of the things I value most about the eldership to which I am privileged to belong is that over the years we have come to the place of speaking the simple truth to one another. I now know that if one of the brothers says something, he means just what the words say; I am not intended to take any unexpressed inference out of it. For my part I am confident that I can say what is on my mind and be sure that the others will not turn it round and round to try and read between the lines or guess what it is I "really" mean. I become aware how little truth speaking like that goes on amongst us, even in marriage and close friendships – "That might be what she said, but I know what she meant."

Not all miscommunication of course is intended, nor is it even conscious. Sometimes what comes out of a person's spirit conveys a different message from the words that come out of the mouth. We need to know how to listen to both messages. Jesus did it superbly. He knew how to listen. Much of our listening is not listening at all if the truth be known. We are just getting our own ideas into shape and waiting for a break in the conversation, so that we can launch them into the space.

If you read the story of Jesus and the Samaritan woman in John 4 you will find a conversation going on at two different levels. When the woman snubbed Jesus, *"You are a Jew and I am a Samaritan woman. How can you ask me for a drink?"* Jesus' reply makes, on the surface, no sense at all. *"If you knew the gift of God and who it is that asks you for a drink, you would have asked him and he would have given you living water."* What was Jesus doing? He was answering the cry from the woman's spirit *"You ask **me** for water? I am the thirsty one."* Again, when she said to Jesus *"You have nothing to draw with and the well is deep . . . "* she was not seeking a discussion on hydraulic engineering. The well was over 400 feet deep into solid rock but her heart was crying, "There is a well of need in me so deep you could drop a stone in and never hear it strike water. How can you meet that emptiness?" That was the question Jesus was answering when he said *"... the water I will give, will become in him a spring of water welling up to eternal life."*

I think I first began to detect this sort of thing when I used to work in the city of Wellington with Teen Challenge. Listening to the kids off the streets and wincing at their scorn and blasphemy of God and Christianity and church and religion, I started to hear something else. Underneath it all there was often a cry that was really saying "Won't *somebody* try to prove me wrong. Isn't there anybody to show me I'm right off the wall and there really is somebody who cares?" I learned to listen under the words and behind the words, and found time and again beneath the sarcasm and invective there was cold naked fear and the anger born of hurt and rejection. Take the spoken words at face value and you have missed communication altogether.

How then can I know what the other person's words really mean? When do I miss the mark because I take them literally and when do I miss the mark because I try to read between the lines and end up reading my own presuppositions?

Self-disclosure, the open door

To know and understand another person in the terms we have been describing is dependent on something else, and that something else is not a matter of communication skills and techniques at all ... it is dependent on the other person's willingness to reveal themself. Knowledge of persons depends on self-disclosure. We understand this perfectly well in relation to God. Our knowledge of God is totally dependent on revelation, that is God's willingness to reveal himself to us. *"Can a man by searching find out God?"* says Job. No he can't. We are dependent on God's willingness to disclose himself to us. Revelation is the divine self-disclosure. Those who want a knowledge of God that does not have to depend on revelation simply do not understand personhood. You cannot even know another human person by reason alone, you are totally dependent on the willingness and the ability of the other person to reveal himself or herself.

85

But such self-disclosure creates a condition of real vulner-ability. There is the risk of hurt and woundedness if I reveal my real self and am then rejected, or criticised, or mocked. Most of us learn very early in life what is involved and many of us resolved away back in childhood that we would never take that risk again. Instead we merely project images of ourselves that we hope will be acceptable to the company we are in. If they are not accepted it doesn't matter too much – we were never "in" the image anyway. We can discard that unsuccessful experiment and try something else.

The difficulty is that I become so used to the image I think it is the real me. I identify myself with it, I don't know how to function without it. But to other people, or at least the ones who are looking for real contact, it has about it the ring of counterfeit. Even when they accept it they somehow know it is not the "real" person they have got hold of.

What creates the circumstances that encourages the other person to risk the vulnerability required for self-disclosure? The prerequisites turn out to be the factors we have aleady described – genuine caring love, affirmation of the person's intrinsic worth and the confidence born of trust. We cannot force our way into such knowledge. In a very real sense we stand helplessly outside the door. All we can do is to create a climate in which the person is willing to take the risk of self-disclosure. But consider this sequence –

- You will never understand the other person unless they reveal themself to you.
- They will never reveal themself to you unless they trust you.
- They will never trust you unless they know you.
- They will never know you unless you reveal yourself to them.

This is a critical point to understand. There is a ready market today for books on communication. Neurolinguistic program-ming, body language, creative questioning and sensitive listening – they all hit the best seller lists because they tap into a deeply felt need. Now the knowledge and practice of communication skills is all to the good, but I have the uneasy feeling that such books are often bought to learn techniques that will give us the edge in the communication contest. Persuasive speaking, power with words, better and more convincing arguments, making friends and influencing people – they can all be used for manipulative and dominating ends. And in personal relationships the desire to dominate or manipulate the other person turns out to be deeply dishonouring.

Real knowledge and understanding of another person comes only out of a deep respect for the integrity of the other *and the willingness to take the same risks as they are called to take.* If I want to know I have to be willing to be known. If I want the other person to reveal himself or herself I have first to take the risk of revealing myself. Only when there is the kind of encounter that says, "This is the real me, you can be safe enough to reveal the real you," does real understanding begin to be born.

Discernment – reading the disclosure

So far we have been dealing with what is disclosed in a communication, in other words a message that is being sent. Note we are using "message" in its widest sense to include not just words but feelings, actions, facial expressions, silences and all the other nuances of behaviour and attitudes involved in personal interaction. For the communication to be successful however, not only does the message have to be true and be accurately sent, the person receiving it has to understand it correctly.

When we receive such a communication, verbal and non-verbal, the first thing that happens is that we form a perception as to what the message means. A perception is an interpretation of what we hear and observe. We say, "She put on a brave face but underneath she is really hurting," or "He made a joke of it but you can tell he's mad as hops." Clearly if our perception is mistaken we will get the message wrong, therefore the question of discernment becomes critical, particularly in interpreting the emotional or spiritual factors involved.

What is discernment? Discernment is experienced often as something intuitive, a kind of sixth sense, but in its operation it is actually a process whereby we:

1. Make a preliminary assessment about some matter or other, and
2. Evaluate that assessment against a reliable norm or standard to which we have access so as to arrive at a correct judgment.

For example in my schooldays we had to read a lot of the great English novelists, dramatists and poets. The educational theory was that if you read enough good literature you will get a deposit in your mind as to what good literature is like, so that later when you read a story or an article you will "know" whether it is good writing or not. The same process applies in art, and music. In other words in discernment I first decide whether I like something or not, and secondly I decide whether or not I ought to like it on the basis of the standards of excellence I have absorbed.

Exactly the same process is involved in the discernment of people or situations, and here also we need to develop the accuracy and reliability of our discernment. The steps are as follows:

1. Build up a body of knowledge by becoming aware of your own inner states and reflecting on them. When you experience fear, joy, anger, despair, grief, confusion and so on, take conscious note of what they feel like and how they affect your thinking, your behaviour and your physical state. Add to that personal knowledge by what you can learn from other people's experiences.
2. In relating to people, learn to become aware in your spirit of the other person's inner states, and to identify or assess their feelings, moods, thoughts and reactions.
3. Evaluate your conclusions, that is judge what you sense is the case against what you know from your personal body of knowledge. For example is what I sense really enthusiasm or is it a worked up excitement, or even fear? How does it compare with the way I experience these feelings?
4. Amend or adjust your discernment, if need be, in the light of further knowledge or fuller disclosure or better information.
5. Review your discerning process so as to keep improving it. Ask yourself, "Why did I get it wrong that time?" "Why did I get it right that time?"

Imagination – entering the other's frame of reference

Any message that we communicate, especially any significant message about ourselves, is necessarily affected by our individual frame of reference. Our frame of reference is somewhat akin to a world view, it is the perspective from which we interpret the world around us and what happens to us. It is made up of such things as our value system, the things, activities and relationships that occupy our time or are important to us, our age, our skills, our learning and past experiences, and our individual interests, motivations, opinions and biases and so on. Obviously the person who receives the message also has a frame of reference through which any message he receives is filtered, but unless they understand each other's frame of reference, the understanding of the message will inevitably be distorted.

A young woman, from a large family and gregarious by nature, who is now the mother of two small children, one physically handicapped, and is herself in poor health and living in a new housing area away from all her friends, has a different frame of reference from her husband who was an only child, has a high pressure job in the city, is studying part time to finish his degree and is a player-coach in the local Rugby Football club. To enter the other's frame of reference requires imagination and serious effort, both intention and attention. It means listening so that we hear the other's point of view without countering it or offering explanations, seeking only to stand in their shoes and see things through their eyes.

Empathy

As well as listening there is the question of empathy. Empathy is the ability to put ourselves in the other person's place so that we feel our way into what he or she is feeling.

This is particularly important in marriage and family rela-tionships or close friendships, where intimacy and emotional involvement run high. Husbands need to learn about this. It took me years in our marriage to discover that when a woman says, "We have a problem we need to talk about" she means some-thing quite different to what a man means when he says, "We have a problem we need to talk about." Generally the man means "Let's describe the problem, let's find the answer, let's fix the problem." But what a woman generally means is, "Here's how I feel about it, how do you feel?" Many couples think the answer to their problems is to sit down and talk them over but somehow they end up with more frustration than before they started to communicate. If one person is looking for understanding and response at the emotional level and the other is addressing the situation at an intellectual level they are going to miss each other entirely.

But there is more to it even than that. Most of the words and expressions we use carry an emotional freight, but that payload varies from person to person. In communication the thing we are least aware of is the emotional content of our speech and the non-verbal communication that goes with it – the tone of our voice, the look in our eyes, or the way we stood when we said it. Experiments have shown that the non-verbal content of our communication is far more powerful than the verbal message we send. If the two conflict, the hearer is five times more likely to believe the non-verbal content.

What is the answer to such baffling statistics? We can never get the message infallibly correct short of speaking in mathematical equations. The answer is to establish and maintain relationships at the level of spirit. That bond is strong enough to make light work of the complexities of communication so that we grow in understanding and mutual appreciation by the very process of unscrambling messages. And it works. You get to the place where a glance across the other side of the room, the tilt of an eyebrow, the sag of shoulders or a passing touch can tell you enough about the beloved to fill the pages of a book.

References

1. 1 Corinthians 13:12.
2. Genesis 3:10.
3. John 10:5.
4. Genesis 1:27; 2:18.
5. Genesis 1:22, 28.
6. Genesis 2:23.

Chapter 7

What Damages Relationships?

Relationships can gather stress and begin to founder either because we persist in doing things that hurt the relationship or because we fail to do the things that are necessary to keep it alive and well. Our sins, in other words, may be sins of commission or sins of ommission.

I remember speaking to a woman devastated by the abrupt collapse of a marriage of 20 years. Her husband came home from work one night and said, "It's over. I'm off and I won't be back." She couldn't understand it. She said, "We never had rows or fights. We never even had major disagreements." I think the relationship had long since withered and died just through sheer lack of interest or attention.

The trouble is that sins of ommission are hard to recognise and harder still for us to admit. Our conscience, for example, is not very sensitive to the things we don't do that we should do. It is much more effective at pointing out the things we are doing that we should not be doing. I've heard men say, "I don't beat my wife, I don't waste all my money at the pub, I don't go round with other women," as though that automatically proved that they were all that a husband should be. We have to realise that the inputs that a relationship needs do not happen automatically and they do not take place by default. We have to attend to them deliberately, consciously and consistently for them to produce results.

But obviously there are certain wrong attitudes and forms of behaviour that are highly detrimental to the growth of healthy relationships and it is to some of these that we now turn. Often we do not take them seriously enough until it is too late to reverse the damage. Studying them may alert us to areas where we are failing or may heighten our sensitivity to the impact of our attitudes and actions on our relationships with other people. We will relate these problem areas to the four relationship factors we have been dealing with.

Things that wound love

Love is the closest of all the relationship factors to the emotions, although as we have seen all love is not necessarily emotional love. Because of its proximity to our feelings however, love is the most sensitive of the factors although it is also the most enduring. Love, the Song of Songs says, is as strong as death; it burns like a blazing fire. *"Many waters cannot quench love. Rivers cannot wash it away."*[1]

What then are some of the specific attitudes or forms of behaviour that wound love or make it difficult for love to persist and grow? The **first, we would have to say, is cruelty**. One of the hardest things for us to understand about the human race as we see it today is its cruelty, the terrible things people do to each other. And yet, instinctively we realise that this cruelty is some-how a perversion. We do not call it man's humanity to man, we call it inhumanity. Somehow we know it is not the way man was originally created to be.

Cruelty is inflicting pain on the other person, either carelessly, not caring whether they suffer or not, or deliberately with the intention that the other person suffers. Therefore there is a moral unfeeling about cruelty. A surgeon deliberately inflicts pain when he operates but pain and suffering are not his purpose. The reverse is the aim, the pain is an inevitable but temporary result of actions that aim to relieve suffering. Similarly a parent who disciplines a child or a coach who pushes the athletes to the pain barrier have a beneficent purpose beyond the pain. Cruelty intends merely that pain be felt, that the victim suffers. It is driven by a lust for power or a lust for revenge.

Cruelty may involve physical violence and abuse or it may be psychological or emotional bullying that is just as devastating although it leaves no discernible bruises. There are battered wives and battered children who have never had a hand laid on them. There are battered parents and battered husbands in the same category.

It is very difficult for love to live in a relationship where there is cruelty because cruelty and love are poles apart. Cruelty is as destructive to the love of the perpetrator as it is to the love of the victim. You can no more go on loving the person you are cruel to than you can go on hating a person to whom you are doing good. Thus cruelty is never mollified, the very helplessness of its victims often increases its hatred for them.

Second, there is dislike, that is, feelings of distaste or aversion or repugnance towards the other person. Love as a feeling attracts us towards the object or person that arouses it; dislike is a feeling that repels us from the object or person. Where dishy like is felt or expressed in a relationship it wounds love because it is love's antithesis. Therefore if I persist in doing or saying things that I know the other person dislikes I am inevitably sowing difficulties for our relationship.

Third, there is rejection. Rejection is the spurning or refusal of an offer of, or a request for, closeness and intimacy. A person only feels rejected when they have, in some way, taken an initiative in the direction of intimacy but the approach has been ignored or rebuffed; I do not feel rejected by people with whom I have no desire to be intimate.

Rejection may be motivated by fear, or by our unwillingness or even inability to respond to a proffered relationship that involves somebody getting close to us. For people who have become very shut in on themselves, the approach of intimacy, even the loving offer of intimacy can appear very threatening. Their rejection of it is a defensive reaction, they want and yet at the same time dread people coming close to them.

Particularly when it happens in emotionally charged relationships like marriage, family and personal friendships, rejection is a very hurtful experience that can leave a person deeply wounded. It is always perceived as personal because I have offered myself and it is not my possessions but my person that has been turned down.

Fourth, there is withdrawal or coldness. This is also a form of rejection but is generally more deliberate and intentional. Behind it is often the drive for power because in a relationship with an emotional content the person who is least committed to the relationship or who is least involved emotionally wields the greater power. He or she can draw back at little emotional cost and keep the other person dangling over the cliff edge until they are ready to pay any price to salvage the relationship. Sometimes it is done in a very calculating and cynical way, mixing times of warm acceptance with periods of cold withdrawal just to let the other party know "I could walk out of this any time I chose and then where would you be?"

On the other hand withdrawal may also be a defensive response or reaction to rejection or hurt. Rather than confront the situation or face the prospect of conflict the person merely opts out of the situation altogether or raises defensive walls to keep the other party at a safe distance.

Fifth, ingratitude is hard for love to bear. Ingratitude is taking what we can get from the other person without appreciation or thanks, sometimes without even the recognition that thanks would be appropriate. When we begin to take the relationship, or the people in a relationship for granted, ingratitude soon creeps in. It springs from our monumental self-centredness and in Paul's estimation is, along with lack of respect, one of the factors in man's primal sin. *"For even when they knew God, they did not honour him as God neither were they thankful."*[2]

Ingratitude is probably one of our least attractive failings, lacking any graces whatsoever. It expresses an unwillingness to feel any sense of obligation towards the goodness or generosity of other people; it is getting without any intention of giving anything in return.

Sixth, there is neglect, the classic sin of ommission as far as love is concerned. Neglect, like ingratitude, begins by taking the relationship for granted, but it then goes on to presume on its long suffering and willingness to forgive. Neglect kills love by disappointment, by a process of slow starvation, it is care-less, inattentive, indifferent, and negligent. All the things that love is and love requires, neglect is not.

Neglect occurs at different levels and in different ways. The material welfare of children or other helpless people can be neglected. More often it is the emotional or the spiritual or the relational needs that are neglected. We are spirit beings and we do not live on bread alone. The inability to meet the other person's needs always leaves a lack but is not always blame-worthy. Neglect is always blameworthy because it means that the person could have done something about it but didn't care enough to make the effort. That is what is wounding about neglect.

Seventh, is envy, that is ill will at the success, popularity, privileges or achievements of the other person. Envy is different from jealousy although the words are often used interchangeably. Jealousy wants the position or the possession or the place that you have to be mine also. Envy is darker and deadlier, it is satisfied only when what you have is destroyed so that neither of us will have it. It was envy that motivated the high priests to plot the death of Jesus. Love delights in the success and well being of the other, envy is its absolute antithesis. Envy is endemic in our modern society and the source of much of its strife and division.

Finally, there is meanness that makes it extraordinarily difficult for love to flourish. It is hard to love where there is meanness, not just stinginess or tightfistedness with money, but meanness of spirit. It comes out in pettiness, spitefulness and small mindedness in thoughts and actions. The large heartedness of love has a hard time living with such cramped and cramping attitudes.

Things that breach trust

If love is the most rugged and most enduring of the elements that go to make up a relationship, then trust is certainly the most fragile. Moreover, once trust is lost it is not easily restored, if indeed sometimes it can ever be restored at all. And its restoration always takes time. An offence can be forgiven in a moment, but for the person to trust again is something else, and for the person who has failed to be able to prove that they are now trustworthy is equally difficult. Therefore, trust and trustworthiness need to be cared for and guarded very diligently. To remain bound by love to a person you can no longer trust is probably the most vulnerable position of all in a relationship.

What are some of the things that will damage the bond of trust or make trust difficult? **One is breach of confidence.** *"He that repeats a matter, separates intimate friends"*, says the book of Proverbs.[3] Few things are more destructive of trust in a relationship than to find that something shared in confidence with an intimate friend is now common knowledge. You are unlikely to repeat the same error again but you will undoubtedly have the agony of wondering what else of your inner thoughts and matters of the heart have also been gossipped about.

In some relationships the matter of keeping confidences is of primary importance. Professional advisors, such as doctors or lawyers, counsellors, ministers and priests occupy positions of trust. Confidentiality is presumed in everything that is shared with them in their professional or ministerial capacity. In the more ordinary relationships however, confidentiality is also important but there is always the possibility of genuine misunderstanding. One party assumes that what is shared will be held in confidence, the other party assumes that it is being released for general consumption. The rule is, always check with the confider. If I do not share with others something that I could well have done there is seldom anything lost. But if I share something and unknowingly breach confidence there will undoubtedly be problems and something important, a friend's trust, may be lost. Similarly it is foolish for us to commit ourselves to keep a confidence, before we know the content of the disclosure.

Secondly, there is the matter of unfaithfulness or disloyalty, that is, breaking the terms of the relationship or the obligations that go with it. The heart of the marriage relationship, for example, is covenant. Covenant is a bond of loyalty between two parties. Anything that breaches that bond of loyalty breaks the covenant and strikes at the very core of the relationship. In marriage we understand this in terms of say sexual faithfulness, but other more common forms of disloyalty are also damaging, if not to the same immediately fatal degree. One of the worst is speaking against one another or complaining about the other party behind his or her back. Few things more readily destroy trust in friendships or marriages or working relationships. One of the rules of the early Moravian communities dealt effectively with this problem. If you heard someone who was not present being spoken against you were obligated to go and tell that person what was being said in his or her absence. I wonder how many churches or communities would have the courage to institute a rule like that, but what a healthy effect it would have on all forms of gossip and backbiting.

Disloyalty is particularly devastating because it usually takes place at times of critical vulnerability or exposure. When things got bad, the other person wasn't there, or worse, took sides against us.

Third, betrayal. Disloyalty and betrayal are both abandoning our promised commitment, or sacrificing the trust placed in us. The particular darkness of betrayal is that it is done for personal gain. Peter's sin, when he abandoned Jesus in the hour of his need, was disloyalty, Judas did it for 30 pieces of silver, his was betrayal.

Fourth, dishonesty in all its forms is highly destructive of trust. How can I trust somebody if I cannot be sure that what they tell me is the truth or that they will not cheat or take an unfair advantage of me? This is what bedevils and distorts most of our industrial relations; they start from a basic presupposition that the other party cannot be trusted.

One of the more common ways however in which we are often dishonest and yet get away with it, is making promises and then not keeping them. It seems to me that one of the most difficult concepts for people today, young people in particular, to understand is that a promise is a promise. It is binding; it commits us to the undertaking or course of action even if it proves more costly or more inconvenient than we had anticipated. Situational ethics too often gives us a ready "let out", because circumstances have changed, the promise no longer applies. There is almost a standard rider attached to promises we make today that says, "I promise ... provided always that I do not change my mind or discover more compelling reasons to act differently." We need to rediscover the moral imperative of keeping promises.

But why are they binding, why is it wrong to break a promise? It is wrong to break a promise because God is a God of covenant, he is a faithful God. Therefore just as a lie is an offence against God's truthfulness, a broken promise is an offence against his faithfulness. To break the moral law is not just to break one of God's rules, it is to offend against his nature or character.

Fifth, we cause very similar difficulties for trust by things like unreliability, inconsistency, carelessness and thoughtlessness. Trust requires that I can predict the other person's responses or behaviour with some accuracy; I can depend on him or her abiding by certain consistencies. If I cannot, then trust is very tentative. The same is true for **moodiness** which is unreliability or unpredictability in emotional or feeling states. It is hard to trust someone whose moods are inconsistent. You cannot depend on it that they will feel the same way about things today as they did yesterday.

Sixth, moral weakness is a fatal flaw as far as trust is concerned. It is difficult to trust someone when you have doubts as to whether they have the backbone to stand up under pressure or against opposition, or where they evidence character flaws or lack of principle. This aspect is critical in all important relationships. In pre-marriage counselling, somewhere along the way I have to ask the blunt question, "Do you have enough confidence in this man (or this woman) to trust the rest of your life into his (or her) hands?" I find it takes some of the couples aback – they have never seriously thought about the question. Yet character is all important when the pressure comes on. No woman wants a man who won't be around when there are problems; and no man wants a woman who is likely to collapse in floods of helpless tears when the crises arrive.

Character is doubly critical when it comes to the relationship between people and their leaders. What, for example, do people have to trust in leaders? For one thing, they have to trust the leader's judgment, that the leader has both got the right goal and has got the goal right. Then they are also trusting in the leader's resourcefulness, that is that when in the future they are faced with as yet unknown situations they have it in them to make the right decisions and the right choices. But they are also trusting the leaders' integrity, that is, that if the leaders make a mistake they will not try to cover it up or evade responsibility but will face up to their error and lead the people back on to safe ground. And they are also trusting the leaders' perseverence, that they will hang in there even when the going gets tough. If people get the idea that their leaders are likely to bale out and take care of their own skins if things go wrong they will hesitate to follow them very far. And they will be right. Faithfulness, particularly steadfastness in the face of trials and difficulties is an essential factor in the character of a leader.

Seventh, lack of self-confidence. In other words, "How can I be sure of you when you are not sure of yourself?" This is particularly important in leaders, fathers and other authority figures. Sometimes in an organisation, a church for example, things seem to be going well on all sides, but you sense an undercurrent of uneasiness among the people. What is often the case is that they are picking up the inner uncertainty of their leaders. Leaders in any organisation are there to provide the source of courage and confidence for their people that will carry them through the bad times. If that is lacking, trust will be tenuous at best, *"their confidence is fragile and their trust like a spider's web."*

Eighth, unfairness or injustice. "I can't be sure of getting a fair deal." This is also critical for leaders. When a person's responses or decisions are affected by favouritism, prejudice, bias, discrimination or other distortions we cannot trust their judgments because they are based on hidden irrational or emotive agendas.

Finally, we need to mention jealousy here because jealousy stems very often from lack of trust. A person is afraid or wary of being supplanted in the affections of the other party or of losing a privileged position or a valued goal. Jealousy breeds suspicion and engenders rivalry and bitterness. Where it is not warranted it is particularly difficult for the other party to live with or to defuse, because nothing he or she says or does can somehow reassure the jealous partner. Jealousy, like inferiority, somehow manages to feed on and live off the very assurances that seek to dispel it.

> *"Anger is cruel and fury is overwhelming,*
> *But who can stand before jealousy?"*[4]

Things that damage respect

Once we begin to realise the importance of respect and honour in relationships and what is involved in them we often become painfully aware of our failures in this area. Attitudes and actions that actually dishonour the other person have often crept into the relationships that mean most to us or those that form the greatest part of our life. Worldly wisdom even seems to nourish that expectancy. Familiarity, we are told, breeds contempt, idols have feet of clay, no man is a hero to his valet. It seems to say, in effect, that the more you know of a person, the less respect you will have for that person. We will come back to this later.

We also begin to identify more clearly the real feelings that sometimes lie behind our anger or resentment or hurt over relational problems – we are aware of being somehow dishonoured. We are treated not as individuals with worth and value but on a par with the furniture, or worse still "like dirt". The problem is lost dignity.

Here are some of the common attitudes or behaviour patterns that can damage respect, or make it difficult for a person to maintain his or her self-respect.

Things that make it difficult for people to respect us
First, there is inadequacy, incompetence and repeated failure. Failure does not of itself endanger other people's respect for us, or even our own self-respect, unless it is in an area in which we have claimed to be competent, or one that is essential to the task we have to undertake. I am not likely to lose people's respect for me because I am no good at map reading. But if I claim to be an expert and lead a tramping party into the bush, only to get thoroughly lost, I am likely to lose their respect for me as a guide quite rapidly.

Similarly, if we give a situation our very best shots but still fail, we are unlikely to lose people's respect. They will say, "Well, at least he tried hard." But if our efforts are usually half-hearted or perfunctory people are going to find it difficult to have respect for us.

Second, irresponsibility, that is, when a person seeks to gratify his own desires with no thought of the affect his actions have on other people, or when he seeks to evade responsibility for the consequences of his actions by "passing the buck" or blaming somebody else. Irresponsible conduct soon loses people's respect.

Third, selfishness. History has no evidence of any human society that has admired the selfish person. Some have admired the proud man, the cruel man, even the treacherous man, but never the selfish man. Selfishness and self-seeking, particularly when a person uses his position as leader to accomplish his own ends rapidly lowers him in people's estimation.

Fourth, self-indulgence and self-pity. There is sometimes a certain reluctant admiration for the strong self-sins like pride and arrogance, but never for the weak ones like self-indulgence and self-pity, particularly in leaders who are soft on themselves, take advantage of their position to avoid discomforts and hardships their people have to go through, or who bemoan their lot and fall prey to the "poor me" syndrome when the going gets tough.

Fifth, moral failure. Here we are not speaking about the fallenness with which all of us are tainted and against which the very best of Christians still have to strive. But there are some areas of moral failure considered particularly dishonourable, especially in leaders or those who hold positions of prominence or responsibility. They include:

(a) Moral weakness or the inability to stand up under pressure. This is seen when we abandon our stated principles because of opposition, or in order to protect ourselves, or because keeping them is too costly. Conversely we respect anybody who has the courage of their convictions.

(b) Breaking promises, particularly serious vows like marriage vows, or encouraging or tempting someone else to break their vows. Keeping one's promises was once a matter of honour, we still say, "Word of honour" or we "honour" our undertakings. Breaking our word is not only a breach of trust, it is a slight on our honour.

(c) Dishonesty and all forms of deceitful, fraudulent or hypocritical behaviour.

(d) Unfairness, injustice, partiality and favouritism, particularly when committed by people who are in positions of power or leadership or who do it for personal gain or advantage.

Finally, there is pettiness in all its forms – the husband who makes a fuss over the way his eggs are cooked for breakfast, the wife who sulks every time she doesn't get her own way, the friend who is mortally offended because you didn't answer her last letter or the deacon who wants to resign because somebody forgot to tell him a meeting had been cancelled. When minor or insignificant issues are blown up out of all proportion we recognise something small or insignificant about the person who does it. That smallness we find difficult to respect or admire.

Attitudes that are dishonouring towards the other person
First in importance is when people are used as a means to an end, instead or being an end in themselves. How we go about using people for our own ends varies widely. We may dominate by sheer force of will, or use various forms of social, religious, psychological or emotional pressure or other forms of duress or blackmail. We may do it more subtly by manipulation or persuasion or politicking or pressure groups.

When workers get the impression that management really

regards them as little more than breathing robots or expendable economic cannon fodder you have a certain recipe for industrial strife. When a wife comes to the conclusion that all she is to her husband is someone to look after the kids and cook the meals and go to bed with, you have a marriage that is already in deep trouble.

Secondly, criticism, nagging and fault finding are damaging to a person's sense of personal worth or value. I remember a father at a men's retreat confessing with tears that he had driven both his sons away from home because he had never done anything but find fault with them from the time they were little boys. Doubtless his intention had been good but the message he had conveyed to his boys was one about their worthlessness.

Often we are only too ready to believe the worst about ourselves and when this is articulated by those who are important in our lives, it confirms our worst fears. It can become a literal curse, a ban or blight on our whole life.

Allied to this is the tendency we sometimes have to embarrass the other person or to put them down in front of people, sometimes in the guise of humour. There are few things more painful than to hear a husband ridicule his wife's opinions in front of others, or criticise her efforts or poke fun at her in a way that embarrasses her. When that happens there is a relationship heading for the rocks, if it is not already on them. Contrast this with Proverbs 31:29, the husband's outburst of pride towards his wife – *"Many women have done nobly, but you surpass them all."*

The fault is not restricted to husbands and wives, parents do it with children, and sometimes children with parents or with other children, it can happen in the workplace or the classroom and not infrequently on the speaker's platform.

Equally devastating although less easy to sheet home is being ignored or disregarded. When our opinions receive no response at all, or our presence goes unacknowledged or our wishes are not so much rejected as not regarded as worth considering, we feel dishonoured – a nothing and a nobody. Children feel little strangers in their own homes, wives feel on the level of the kitchen appliances; it is the end result of a creeping paralysis that probably set in years ago.

Discourteous and disrespectful speech and behaviour in all its forms. It is particularly blameworthy, because it is particularly hurtful, when rude, careless or demeaning speech or attitudes are expressed towards those who are least able to defend themselves, for example, the poor, the elderly, the young or the helpless.

Another is parading the other person's failures or weaknesses in public or before others. There is great courtesy as well as great wisdom in the biblical injunction, that if your brother sins against you, you are to go and show him his fault just between the two of you. Where people have to be corrected or their mistakes pointed out, it should always be done in private. You are much more likely to get improvement when you try to protect the person's self-esteem even though you have to deal very directly with his failures.

Talking down to people or treating them as incompetents. This is the disparaging attitude that either refuses to explain or discuss a matter with people because they are not considered clever enough, or educated enough to understand, or else goes into over-elaborate and pedantic explanations of simple matters that show what we think of the level of intelligence of the hearers.

In all the above ways, and in others, disrespect and dishonour can be communicated. Sometimes it is deliberate and overt or done openly; sometimes it is deliberate but covert or underhand; and sometimes it is done unconsciously. The message of dishonour however, whether explicit or implicit is always damaging and often devastating because it calls into question the value and worth, and the sense of significance of those towards whom it is directed.

Barriers to understanding

We come now to consider some of the things that can cause misunderstanding in relationships or make understanding difficult. We are not so much concerned with what the common misunderstandings are but with the more fundamental issue of how they happen in the first place.

Mutual knowledge and understanding depends on two things; they depend on conveying accurate and meaningful disclosures about ourselves, and they depend on making accurate and meaningful interpretations of the disclosures that the other person is making of himself or herself.

   The first and most common barrier to understanding is therefore, lack of communication or inadequate communication. It is very difficult, if not impossible, for the other person to understand us because they are forced to rely on perceptions based on inadequate or non-existent information. Their conclusions are thus inferences or guesses as to the real nature of the person we are. True, there is communication of a sort going on all the time. Even our silences communicate something. But unless we are able to convey our thoughts, our fears, our feeling states and our opinions in ways that are understood, the possibility of mis-understanding escalates.

Inadequate or imperfect communicating can be due to a number of causes

Shyness or reserve. This may be a temperamental difficulty in expressing our inner life or it may be that we lack the confidence to trust ourself to people even in conversation because we have never learned to do so as children. Or it may be an even more unhealthy secretiveness because there are hidden things in our desires and thoughts that we dare not bring out into the light of day. This prevents us from speaking because we are afraid that the wrong things might leak out.

   Feelings of inferiority, insecurity, inadequacy, or other inhibitions may have convinced us that we have nothing of value to give and that no one would be interested in our disclosures anyway. Because of this we either do not communicate at all, or we do so in such a stilted and inept manner that it is likely to be disregarded or overlooked, which confirms us in our feelings.

   Lack of self-knowledge or self-awareness. Young children cannot tell us a lot about themselves because before a certain age they lack any great degree of self-awareness. When mother asks Johnny in exasperation, "Tell me why you did that" and Johnny looks blank and says, "I dunno" he is probably telling the whole truth. He doesn't yet really know anything much about his own inner self. Severely emotionally deprived adults often have the same difficulty.

   Having an image of the other person as aloof or rejecting. This can happen in the relationship between children and parents, especially fathers, between people and leaders, pupils and teachers and other authority relationships. The powerful influence is the image we have of one another, even if the image is in fact wrong, and oftentimes we are unaware of the image we project towards people.

Lack of time or opportunity to communicate. This is very common in marriage and family relationships. It takes time to communicate and if necessary we need to discipline ourselves to set aside blocks of time to learn and practice how to communicate with each other. In allocating our time, the urgent things should never get priority over the important things, and in terms of intimate relationships, communication is high priority on the list of important things.

Differing perceptions as to the level of intimacy appropriate to the relationship. This is common in church fellowships or small groups, where the expectation as to how open the relationship is meant to be can vary from one participant to another. What may be taken as a lack of openness in some people may merely be that they do not regard the relationship as involving a degree of intimacy that warrants such personal sharing of themselves.

Emotional woundedness or hurt from previous relationships. This creates extreme vulnerability to the prospect of being rejected and makes the self-disclosure needed for understanding seem like a terrifying ordeal.

Differences in age, sex, education, social status or culture, can also stand in the way of communicating effectively with one another.

Deception. Sometimes the other person is trying to deceive us, or we are trying to deceive them. Often we are trying to create an impression that is not really in accord with reality – there is deception there also, no matter how innocent or harmless it may seem. And there is the extreme case of the person who is self-deceived. They believe ardently in what they are communicating but have so lived with untruth that they do not even know that it is falsehood.

Finally, there are all the various forms of mistake, misconception and miscommunication to which we are prone. No communication is error free. With the best will in the world and with the most skilled techniques being used we can still misunderstand, even foolishly misunderstand each other. Such miscomprehension is the stock in trade of the comic, in real life, the outcomes are sometimes less than humorous.

Even when the information or messages that people communicate about themselves are accurate and revealing, there can be problems caused by the way in which the communication is received

Problems in perception can arise from:

The effect of bias, prejudice and dogmatism. These are all examples of opinions arrived at beforehand without reason or without having all the facts. The message is therefore either blocked by a mind that is already made up or is taken to mean something quite different from what was intended by the speaker.

Similar in effect are **hasty judgments or jumping to conclusions** without hearing the full story.

Insensitivity or lack of imagination, can also cause distortion because the hearer is unable to enter the speaker's frame of reference, while **lack of empathy** can lead to a mistaken interpretation of the other person's feelings.

The inability or unwillingness to listen properly is the cause of much of the misunderstanding and misinterpretation that goes on in communication. Listening, as opposed to waiting for the other person to run out of breath so that we can have our say, is hard and sacrificial work. Maybe that is why we do not do it very much.

Finally, there is the different association or emotive content given to words by different people. Because of our past experiences certain words come to have emotional overtones or associations, quite apart from the literal or figurative meaning of the words themselves. These associations are largely unconscious, all we are aware of is that certain words "feel" threatening, or unclean, or domineering, or sarcastic. We are of course totally ignorant of the associations or emotive content they have for the other person.

What is the answer?

This chapter may leave us with the impression that the whole business of relationships is such a minefield that our chances of getting through successfully are very slight indeed.

Thankfully that is not the case. Furthermore we will do far better by putting our major efforts into building the strengths of our relationships than by concentrating all our attention on correcting their weaknesses. To have four chapters on the positive factors and one on the negative is probably somewhere about the right balance.

Nevertheless we need to be aware of the potential hazards because they surely are there and it is generally when we have been slack in cultivating the relationship that the defects are likely to creep in. We will deal with problem solving more fully in a later chapter but one or two comments are helpful here if we have become aware that we have been guilty of some of the wrong attitudes mentioned above.

The solution always begin with a frank admission of our failure and the nature of our failure but it also requires that we take pains to correct it. That will generally mean consciously adopting the opposite attitude or spirit to the one we have been expressing. All evil is essentially negative or the absence of good; criticism is the absence of affirmation and appreciation, rejection is the absence of acceptance and intimacy and so on. Therefore we need to compensate, and often for a time, over-compensate for what we have done. If I have greatly discouraged a staff member or a friend or a spouse or a child by my negative attitude I have to realise that there is a deficit I have to make up in the relationship. I will need to be more than ordinarily encouraging to overcome and repair the damage I have caused. If I have broken trust, I have to accept the responsibility of patiently and consistently rebuilding that confidence again until it takes hold.

Properly used, evidence of where we have been failing can give us a clearer idea of what we need to attend to in a relationship. If I have failed in areas affecting understanding, that is what I need to work on, not more trust or more respect. If I have been guilty of things that wound love, again it is not more understanding or knowledge that is needed, it is more care and more affection.

References

1. Song of Songs 8:7.
2. Romans 1:21 ASB.
3. Proverbs 16:28 ASB.
4. Proverbs 27:4.

Chapter 8

When Relationships Break Down

A breakdown in any relationship that we value is always stressful and the stress experienced is usually in direct proportion to the importance of the relationship.

The greater the degree of intimacy in a relationship, the greater is the trauma involved if it comes apart. The greater the scope or area of our life affected by a relationship the greater is the upheaval if the relationship is severed.

The two aspects are not necessarily the same. A drastic change in vocation may involve considerable upheaval in our lifestyle and a major reordering of relationships but there may be very little trauma involved. There will still be a considerable degree of stress because of the extent of the changes that take place.

On the other hand the fracturing of an intimate friendship or the loss of a family relationship by bereavement may be very traumatic although the outward pattern of our life alters very little. One of the features of marriage breakdown is the compounding of both trauma and upheaval that makes it particularly damaging. I spoke recently to a woman who at different times in her life had know the pain of divorce and the pain of bereavement in a subsequent marriage. She ranked the suffering of divorce as far greater than that of bereavement. "In my second marriage," she said, "I lost my husband but I never lost his love and I know that one day we will be reunited. But in my first marriage I lost my husband and I lost his love as well, that is what made it so hard."

Mental states

Under stress our judgment is liable to be clouded and the quality of our decision-making impaired. It is essential to remember this when trying to help people caught in the middle of relational problems, or if we are in that situation ourselves. We therefore need the corrective of a wise, impartial voice from outside, from someone who is concerned but is not personally or emotionally involved in the problem.

We have all observed a person we used to think was so balanced and objective suddenly become dogmatic, bigoted and obtuse towards a spouse or someone with whom they have to work closely. They are not necessarily acting deliberately or wilfully in this way, they may merely be showing some of the common results of stress in relationships.

Here are some of the states of mind that we are likely to meet or experience when relationships break down.

One is **self-justification** – "It wasn't my fault." This is the tendency to see ourselves as being in the right in the dispute or being the injured party or the innocent victim of the other person's ill will or ill behaviour. The capacity of the human heart for self-justification and self-deception is almost unlimited, which is why we need the Holy Spirit to search our hearts and open our eyes to the truth. Many times I have found the totally convincing and compelling structure of reasons and arguments that certified my complete innocence come tumbling down like a pack of cards in his presence.

The other side of self-justification is **recrimination** – "It was all your fault." Here, the other person is seen as wholly or mainly to blame for what has happened. Recrimination usually includes not only passing judgment on the person's behaviour but also interpreting their motives. We know "why" they spoke or acted in that way or what was "really" behind their behaviour. It is this kind of judging that Jesus calls into question so severely. Our understanding of our own true motives in notoriously unreliable; we are even more poorly placed to pass accurate judgment on the motives of other people.

Accompanying both these states of mind there usually is a third – **excuse** – "I couldn't help it." This is our need to find reasons that absolve us from blame or responsibility for the way we acted or reacted. We have to find an explanation that will enable us to feel that anybody else in the same circumstances would have done or said or felt just the way we did. Sometimes the blanket of excuse is thrown over both parties to the dispute then we can even salvage some virtue from the wreckage, "I don't blame my husband either, if his father had helped him financially as he should have, he would have had a lot less to contend with."

Finally, particularly common in marriage breakdown is **sheer confusion**. Neither party seems to have any clear idea of what has gone wrong or what caused their difficulties. "We started out so much in love. How on earth did we get ourselves into this mess?" "I don't know what we did wrong. I can't believe it has actually happened to us."

All these mental states are conscious, but there are others which are unconscious and because of that, even more potent. They are the so-called defence mechanisms, used by the ego to protect itself from painful or unpleasant insights.

One example of this kind of ego armour is **rationalisation**. Rationalisation is replacing the real reason by another that is more acceptable to our self-image. For example, we are passed over for promotion at work. We may be convinced that it is because we are a Christian, or female, or coloured, or don't drink with the in crowd, or won't curry favour with the boss. The real reason, that we are just not good enough for the job, may be one that we are totally unable to face. Unconsciously we find more acceptable reasons to explain our failure.

Projection is another common defence mechanism. It is our ability to see faults in other people that are really our own particular failings to which we are totally blind. The person who is always complaining about a critical spirit in the church is likely to be projecting their own problem on those around them. Jesus' parable of the mote and the beam is a classic illustration of projection.

A third is **displacement**. Reactions or feelings that we are unable or unwilling to express or admit in one quarter are given vent to in a totally unrelated situation. The man who is reprimanded or disciplined on the job and suppresses his anger for fear of the boss, or to protect his image at work, may come home and fly into a rage with his wife or children over nothing at all. He will generally be quite unaware of what he is doing,

111

merely amazed that his wife and children can be so unbearably irritating and deliberately provocative when all he was looking forward to was a quiet family evening.

Emotional states

When relationships are under stress or breaking down, a considerable amount of emotional tension and suffering is always involved. People's emotional reactions are very complex and if we are coming into such a situation from the outside we need to be sensitive and discerning as to what is being experienced. Outward manifestations are not enough to go on. For example, a person bursts into tears. Is it grief, joy, guilt, relief, fear, frustration, rage or pain? If we act or react from a misinterpretation of the feelings that are being expressed we can easily make matters worse.

Here are some of the common emotional states experihy enced when important relationships are under pressure or disintegrating.

The first is **pain**. It may be expressed as hurt, loss, grief, sadness, loneliness or depression. The suffering involved in emotional hurt is as painful as any physical wound but because there is little outward evidence, it attracts less sympathy. Anybody can see and make allowances for a broken arm; nobody sees a broken heart. We do not generally counsel a person with a broken leg to pull himself together the way we expect a person with a broken spirit to do.

The second is **anger**. Because anger is wrongly considered by many Christians to be always unacceptable you will often find people claiming to be hurt when in fact they are angry. Besides, hurt may attract sympathy, anger seldom does. Anger may come out as hostility, bitterness, malice, revengefulness or spite. It is never helped by concealing it or misnaming it. We need to understand that anger is a legitimate part of our emotional equipment. It is one of the emergency emotions whose function is to arouse us to face threat or danger. If the issue is not faced or resolved, anger easily slides over into resentment, which literally means "to feel over and over again." We will deal with this aspect of anger in more detail when we talk about problem solving in relationships.

Guilt feelings are in many ways the hardest for us to handle. This is probably why we both consciously and unconsciously, seek to defend ourselves against them. Guilt can manifest itself in three main forms. The first is **regret**, which is a kind of neutral, passive state. The second is **remorse** or **condemnation** which is a negative and unproductive state that readily becomes morbid and mixed with self-pity. The third is **repentance** which can lead to positive amendment. Repentance is not only a sorrow for our wrongdoing but a turning from it with a desire to make restitution and recompense and to rectify our wrong attitudes and behaviour.

A fourth group of emotions cluster around **fear** – they include apprehension, alarm, anxiety, dread and panic. They occur when the comfortable, familiar and secure things are disintegrating. Ahead is the unknown and the unpredictable and the unthinkable. Will I be able to cope? What is going to happen? Anger, guilt and fear usually go hand in hand. If one is in evidence, the others will almost always be around, perhaps just below the surface; they reinforce and activate each other. For example a child is angry with his parents; he feels guilty because he has been taught that he ought to love his parents. Guilt brings fear of punishment or other consequences; fear triggers anger which is a defensive reaction to danger; the anger generates more guilt and the guilt produces more fear. Only when the cycle is broken by forgiveness can release and healing take place.

A fifth state is **jealousy** or **envy**. Jealousy is resentment over the loss of a privileged position, for example, when our place in the other person's life or affections is taken over by someone else. Jealousy persists in many marriages that have ended in divorce to the apparent relief of both parties. To be supplanted, even in a role that you no longer think you want provokes jealous feelings. Envy is the destructive form of jealousy. Jealousy says, "I want what you have," or "I want back what I have lost to you." Envy says, "I would rather destroy it altogether so that neither of us can have it." Envy is one of the particularly damaging emotions on the loose in all levels of our modern society.

Finally, there are feelings of **alienation**, **estrangement**, **apathy** and **indifference**. With the latter of these, the relationship is dead, lacking even the desire for it to be restored. The person just does not care any more. Even the possibility of restoration or reconciliation fails to awaken a quiver of interest.

Behaviour patterns

The basic behaviour patterns that result from these states of mind and feelings can be characterised as either fight or flight, although they may also swing wildly between both extremes. In the former there is conflict, contention, strife and confrontation. It may spill over into aggressive and violent behaviour. There may be physical abuse or even more commonly, emotional and psychological abuse. In the latter there is withdrawal and avoidance of contact altogether; the person just wants out.

In spite of outward appearances, the former state is generally the more hopeful of the two as far as the relationship is concerned. It indicates that at bottom one or both of the parties feels that there is still something in the relationship worth fighting for, even if its only their own self-respect. In the latter, the person has consciously or unconsciously weighed up the pros and cons involved in the relationship and come to the conclusion it is just not worth the effort.

Intervening to help

We have spent some time on what may seem to be the pathology of relationships. Dealing with the mental and emotional states of the people involved is not however, the primary key to healing or restoring the relationship as we will see later. Nevertheless these states represent the minefield we will encounter in seeking to help the people concerned, therefore we need to understand what we are facing. Blundering about in a minefield is not to be recommended.

The way through is not as difficult as we might think, provided we remember one very important fact. *In trying to help another person, whether as counsellor, friend, confidante, or pastor, we are involved in a relationship with them. That relationship needs the same input and the self-same factors as any other relationship.* In other words, we need to concentrate, not on the techniques of handling the person's varying or unpredictable emotional moods or mental states, but on manifesting love, trust, respect and honour and a genuine attempt to understand them and what they are going through.

Take love for example. If we do not genuinely care for the person we will never be able to help them effectively no matter how skilled our counselling techniques may be. People going through the trauma of broken relationships are more than ordinarily sensitised to emotional and spiritual conditions. They will discern and be aware of impatience, disinterest, criticism or condemnation if they are in our heart, no matter how skilfully we dissemble or try to hide them.

It is the same with respect. Because a person is experiencing failure or rejection in an important area of their life, their self-confidence and self-image are under severe threat. They are deeply in need of respect, regard and affirmation to shore up their sense of worth and value. An attitude of superiority on our part or any hasty, simplistic solutions to the problems they face will be interpreted as demeaning them still further. That is why Paul wrote with such wisdom to the Galatians. *"Brethren, if a man be overtaken in a fault, you who are spiritual restore such a one in the spirit of meekness, considering yourself lest you also be tempted."*[1]

In the same way we need to build **an atmosphere of trust and confidence** in which people feel safe enough to let it all hang out knowing that it will go no further and also that it will not be turned and used against them.

Finally the person's first and most desperate need is to find **somebody who wants to understand**; not to agree with them, or approve or take sides but to genuinely try to understand. The very common situation in a severely stressed relationship is to find two people who think they know exactly what is wrong with the other person, who are convinced that the other person doesn't understand them at all, but who don't really understand themselves.

When there is patient, intelligent, sacrificial and caring listening the troubled person can often find the courage to discharge his or her mental confusion and emotional turmoil. When this is done their power subsides, at least temporarily. Pieces of the puzzle may drop into place and some of the hidden issues may emerge into conscious awareness. Then, and then only are they able to hear from somebody else.

References

1. Galatians 6:1–2.

Chapter 9

The Way Back – Reconciliation

It should not be necessary today for anybody to write a book about the need for reconciliation. The need hits us in the face everywhere. Race relations, family relationships, industrial and international relations all exhibit vast amounts of pain, anger, fear, and guilt. They cry out to be healed. Nor is the willingness for reconciliation totally absent, although there are people on both sides of each divide who are driven by fear or prejudice into extremes of antagonism.

The problem is that so often we seem to lack not only the resources to produce true reconciliation but also the methodology. The dynamic to make it possible and the "how-to" to put it into effect both elude us. We talk no end about reconciliation; we even deeply desire it. We try to solve specific grievances and create new ones in the process, but we do not bring about reconciliation, whether in marriage breakdowns; industrial disputes or Ireland, South Africa or the West Bank. We wonder why it does not happen.

I am convinced that a major reason for this situation is our assumption that everybody knows how to be reconciled, if they really want to. So we end up yelling at each other to do it, and get more bitter and alienated in the process. The particular tragedy of modern times is the idea that pressure will move the log jam, the ultimate form of pressure being violence. We end up shooting one another in the cause of reconciliation.

The Bible alone gives the reason for this contradiction between what we want to do and what we end up doing. Its answer is simply that alienation, in all its forms, is one of the primary results of the Fall. In other words, alienation is second nature to our fallen nature. Reconciliation, on the other hand is totally foreign to us and wholly dependent on divine grace.

Christians have an awesome responsibility in a deeply divided world because to us God has given the particular ministry of reconciliation (2 Corinthians 5:18). If, however, we try to reconcile without understanding and using the power of divine grace, we will fail, and fail even more ignominiously than secular counsellors or therapists. Furthermore, if we try to do it without understanding and using the methods God uses, we will fail again. And these failures will be blameworthy, because if our responsibility is the ministry of reconciliation we are obligated to master both its dynamics and its methods.

This section of the book is therefore the most crucial of all. Understand it and a new field of hope in dealing with stressed and broken relationships will open up for you as it did for me. Skip over it because it seems too theological, or rush through it because you think you understand it already, and you will ultimately have to come back to it again and again.

My own search for answers to this dilemma was, I realise, driven by a deep sense of dissatisfaction with the poor record of the Church in restoring stressed or broken relationships. It seemed to me that the achievements of Christian counselling were little better than those of secular counselling and neither record was anything to get excited about.

One Friday afternoon I was sitting in my office reading Ephesians 2. I got down to verse 13 where Paul points out that we *"who once were far away have been brought near through the blood of Christ."* Then he goes on to say *"For he himself is our peace, who has made the two into one and has destroyed the barrier, the dividing wall of hostility ... His purpose was to create in himself one new man out of two, thus making peace ..."* I remember stopping there and thinking, "How on earth can Paul go from discussing salvation to racial discrimination like that, without even stopping for breath?"

Then suddenly I saw what I wish I had seen and ought to have seen years ago, that *the Cross of Christ is the effective means of **all reconciliation**, not only in the relationship between God and the human race but in all the relationships between human beings.*

In other words, the Cross is the answer to all the various forms of alienation and division caused by sin. Every one of the great words used to describe salvation has the theme of restoring something to its original design, or purpose. Thus redemption is buying back something that has gone into slavery, regeneration is giving life back to something that has died, salvation has the sense of salvage, rescuing something from destruction. When it comes to relationships, the word is reconciliation. The Cross is the divine and only resource of unlimited reconciliation. It reconciles not only humanity to God but person to person.

In marriage breakdown, industrial disputes, business antagonism, racial disharmony and international conflict, we find the factors are the same: strife, injustice, oppression, misunderstanding, broken promises, shattered respect. Any solution that does not go to the heart of these issues will never achieve reconciliation.

We may devise solutions, reach compromises, and strike bargains but remain with both sides each intent on giving as little as possible and gaining as many guarantees as possible. What confidence would we have for a marriage "restored" on such a basis?

What is reconciliation?

Reconciliation has two main meanings. It signifies the restoration of accord and harmony between parties who were at odds with one another or it refers to the settling of a dispute or disagreement between parties.

In the New Testament the word *reconciliation is used to describe the total result of Christ's life and death that permanently changed the relationship between God and the human race by changing their attitudes towards each other.*

The aim of reconciliation is therefore the restoration of righteousness. Because of our use of the word justification to describe the process of making righteous we tend to think of righteousness as a legal concept. In fact it is a relational term. It means to be rightly related or in the old English term to be "rightwise". To be made righteous is therefore to be made rightwise with God in a relationship of accord and harmony.

Reconciliation involves a change of attitudes, because attitudes are all important in relationships.

Attitudes differ from beliefs. Beliefs are largely cognitive, that is, they affect the way we think about issues or values. Attitudes have a cognitive element, but in addition they have emotional elements and behavioural elements. We do not generally act on our beliefs, but we do act in accordance with our attitudes. In fact our attitudes are shown by the way we behave.

For example, I may believe that all men are equal regardless of colour or race. But if I am white and do not have any personal friends who are non-whites, my racial attitude shows clearly.

The attitudes both of God and mankind are changed by the Cross. God's attitude to the human race is changed from wrath to blessing; our attitude to God is changed from rebellion and enmity to sonship.

Note carefully that God's feelings towards us have never changed. *God's feeling towards his fallen creatures has always been unconditional, unchanging, infinite love. But God's attitude towards sin must always be holy wrath.* He cannot overlook sin. Sin is an offence which he cannot overlook and remain God the only Holy One.

Let me give an illustration. You are a man and you are walking along a road. If you came across another man beating a woman, you could not just walk by and ignore it. You could not do that and live with yourself, the act is an offence against your manhood. Even if the attacker ran off you would have to go after him and bring him to account for his actions. In a far, far greater degree all sin is an offence against God's "God-ness", therefore he cannot remain aloof and neutral.

Therefore reconciliation necessitates atonement. *Atonement is the covering of sin by something that robs it of its power to permanently disrupt the relationship between collective humankind and God. That "something" is what the New Testament calls the blood of Christ.* The dread of the human race has always been the fear that sin is eternal; once I have sinned I am a sinner and nothing can ever change the fact of my sin. It may seem strange to many people today, but that is only because the sense of sin in our society has been repressed. Below conscious level, guilt rages unappeased and none of our modern rationalisations ever free us from its sting. But can anything ever change the face of sin, or is it as Fitzgerald wrote:

"The moving finger writes; and having writ,
Moves on; nor all your piety nor wit
Shall lure it back to cancel half a line,
Nor all your tears wash out a word of it."

Against that dread and that fatalism stands the Cross of Christ, God's final solution to the guilt problem and the sin problem.

Furthermore, and this point is critical, atonement necessitates judgment. We need to understand the principle that is involved even at the human level. A wrong is never dealt with between two persons in a way that permanently removes the offence and therefore the alienation unless in some way judgement is passed on the wrongdoing. Forgiveness alone will not end the power of sin to poison relationships. Only when sin is judged can its disruptive effects be totally overcome.

Judgment must also be understood and its justice recognised by the wrongdoer before it can be redemptive. Even a child needs to understand the reason for the parent's discipline and in some sense agree with its fairness and rightness or discipline will not function as a corrective; it will either crush or provoke the child, it will make him a conformist or a rebel.

No one, not even the very best of the race can understand and agree with God's perfect justice in expressing holy wrath and eternal judgment against sin. The most mature Christian has a struggle in his or her mind at times as to why God seems to make such a fuss over our harmless little sins. That is because we are so infected with the disease that we cannot understand its deadly nature. Only a sinless Sin-Bearer could totally agree with the absolute rightness and perfect justice of God in dealing with sin as he did on the Cross. Therefore the judgment of God fell on the only place in the whole universe where it could be redemptive, on Christ our Representative and our Substitute, the last Adam, and second Federal Head of the human race.

But man is also at heart an enemy against God, a stranger and a rebel. Between us and God there is a double gulf, the gulf between the infinite Creator and the finite creature and an even greater moral gulf between a holy God and a sinful human race that we had neither the means or the desire to cross. **Therefore**

reconciliation necessitates incarnation. To bridge the gulf God has to get a foothold on both sides of the divide. Fallen men and women cannot change their attitudes towards God. There is no unaffected area in human nature where they can stand to get the leverage to effect a change of heart. Since sin and rebellion have touched every area of human life, no neutral or unaffected areas remain.

In the Incarnation God found the leverage. In his Son, the sinless Son of Man, God found a foothold within humanity to make a change of heart possible.

In the Garden of Gethsemane Jesus took our rebellious, self-centred human will, and in himself broke that will to do the Father's will. *"Not what I will but what you will,"*[1] prayed not once or twice but three times before it was done, and in such a moral and spiritual agony that he sweat as it were great drops of blood. It was not his will that Christ grappled with in Gethsemane; it was ours. So by the Cross and the empty tomb comes the miracle of reconciliation. Rebellious enmity towards God changes to loving obedience, scepticism turns to trust, blasphemy becomes transmuted to worship.

Reconciliation leads to communion. God sends the Spirit of adoption into our hearts crying, *"Abba Father"*[2] until our hearts learn the same cry.

What is reconciled?

So far this is truth we need to deeply ponder but it is still familiar ground. The next question, however is, "What is reconciled by the Cross?" In other words, how do we take the apparent leap from reconciliation that leads to personal salvation to reconciling human discord and strife? What does the Cross have to do with marriage breakdown or church division or industrial strife or racial antagonisms? Colossians 1 leads us to the answer. Verse 16 says, *"For by him"* (that is, Christ), *"all things were created, things in heaven and on earth, visible and invisible ... all things were created by him and for him. He is before all things and in him all things hold together."*

And verse 20 says: *"and through him to reconcile to himself all things, whether things on earth or things in heaven, by making peace through his blood, shed on the cross."*

- All things have been created through Christ.
- All things are held together by Christ.
- All things are reconciled through the blood of Christ.

What does that mean for the human situation we have been considering? *The Cross is the divine intervention in all disputes. It is redemption reaching as far as sin has gone and restoring all that sin has damaged.* It is no accident that sin is recorded as first ruining human relationship with God and then ruining human relationships with each other. In the first family the partnership of equals between man and woman degenerates into domination on one side and manipulation on the other. Brotherly love ends in murder.

The Cross is God reconciling all things to himself. Only the atonement makes us at one again; only the Cross restores.

Love's revival

The Cross is where the eternal, redeeming, measureless love of God is outpoured into the human situation. At the Cross we experience the transforming effect of that love on our personal lives. I remember a friend of mine who before his conversion had been a compulsive gambler saying with a kind of glazed wonder in his eyes, "I loved my wife and I loved my children and I knew my gambling was harming their welfare, but I couldn't stop. Why is it that when love for the family I saw every day of my life couldn't change me, love for Christ whom I have never seen washes out my gambler's craving?"

There is a resource of love in the Cross that can regenerate human love that has been so hurt it has finally died, I have seen it happen with my own eyes. There is enough love in the Cross to cause management to care for the welfare and needs of workers and to cause the workers to care for the welfare of the employers. There is enough love available there to awaken compassionate, generous, caring concern between Jew and Arab, Protestant and Catholic, black and white, Americans or South Africans.

Human love has proved its inadequacy in spite of its best endeavours. In the face of major relational strife it is bankrupt of resources. Divine love that cares out of fulness, not out of need, is our only hope. Calvary makes it available in the marketplace, the political arena or anywhere it is needed. Only through the death and resurrection of Jesus Christ is it possible for my enemy to become my neighbour.

Trust's recovery

What is more it is possible for me to trust again someone in whom I had lost all confidence, to be willing to let the outcome of a situation pass out of my control and into his because I now have faith in him. The Cross is also the ultimate act of faith. Jesus took human trust out to the absolute margins, *"Father, into your hands I commit my spirit"*[3] he cried and stepped into the darkness of divine judgment. The future was out of his control, it was in the Father's hands, and he had made no contingency plans.

The faith with which we trust in Christ we get from Christ, just as the love with which we love him comes from him also. That is why Paul said, *"I live by the faith of the Son of God who loved me and gave himself for me."*

And there is faith enough in the Cross to make those who have failed in the past become trustworthy, the undependable become dependable, the unreliable become faithful. Peter and the disciples prove that. The trusting Christ trusts them all over again. Once more no contingency plans but this time a new faith and a new faithfulness.

I have seen that happen too, suspicion replaced by secure confidence on both sides. I never know which is the greatest miracle, to see God make an unclean person clean or a violent person gentle, or a drunk person sober or a dishonest person honest. Perhaps the last of these is the most difficult but I have seen that too, many times.

Honour restored

Only through the Cross can I honour someone for whom I once had no respect because I did not understand him or his ways. Now I have the empathy and the openness to stand in his shoes and see things through his eyes.

Honour or respect is recognising worth or value, and value we have already seen is always imputed. It was the Son's supreme honouring of the Father.

"Father, everything is possible for you. Take this cup from me. Yet not what I will but what you will."[4]

"Now my heart is troubled, and what shall I say? 'Father save me from this hour?' No, it was for this very reason I came to this hour, Father glorify your name."[5]

The Cross is also the source of Jesus' honour.

"But we see Jesus, who was made a little lower than the angels, now crowned with glory and honour because he suffered death, so that by the grace of God he might taste death for everyone."[6]

But Calvary is also the ultimate value placed on the world by God. *"Since you are precious and honoured in my sight, and because I love you."*[7] The supreme value placed by Paul on people was the fact of the Cross. *"A brother for whom Christ died."*[8] Thus, in the Cross there is a resource that can restore respect that has long since been lost, that can enable us to separate the person from the person's behaviour so that we recognize and affirm the intrinsic worth and value of the person and accord it the honour and dignity it warrants. The Cross can change our perspective in such a way that we see men and women as ends in themselves and never as means to an end. We develop a horror of both domination and manipulation and we relate to the needy and weak and the disadvantaged in ways that deeply respect their humanness.

Understanding reawakened

And finally the Cross is the ultimate revelation of the nature and character of God. It is God's final self-disclosure. I suspect that nothing we will ever learn of God's character in all the ages to come will go beyond that. Every circumstance, every question, and every speculation bows in the end to that revelation. Like Job we cry time and again, *"My ears had heard of you, but now my eyes have seen you, therefore I despise myself and repent in dust and ashes."*[9]

If mutual understanding depends on mutual self-disclosure then there is enabling grace in the Cross to give me both the courage and the ability to let the walls down between us so that I can show my real self to you. Grace and tenderness are released in the Cross so that I can create the acceptance that will give you the courage to dismantle your defences and show your real self to me. Such is the power of the Cross that we cling fast to its revelation of the mercy and faithfulness of God in the face of all the tragedy and distress, pain, hurt and iniquity of the fallen world we live in. In spite of it all we know God is just and good and we remain convinced that his providence is motivated by infinite love and guided by infinite wisdom. If the Cross can accomplish that, then it also has the resource to enable us to begin to understand each other in spite of all the communication and behaviour hurdles that stand in the way.

References

1. Mark 14:36.
2. Galatians 4:6.
3. Luke 23:46.
4. Mark 14:36.
5. John 12:27–28.
6. Hebrews 2:9.
7. Isaiah 43:4.
8. 1 Corinthians 8:11.
9. Job 42:5.

Chapter 10

How Does God Reconcile?

When I got this far in my understanding I began to reflect on the "how to", the methodology of reconciliation. The standard approach to reconciliation is a process of problem solving. The method is simple enough to understand – discover the problem, develop possible solutions, select the best solution, apply the solution, and presto – reconciliation!

The only difficulty is that it doesn't work. The method is very effective for mechanical, organisational and operational problems, but except for the most superficial matters it is almost totally ineffective for interpersonal and racial disharmonies.

To begin with, the problems of a relationship that has been going downhill for a long time are so complex and tangled it is virtually impossible to unravel them so as to get at the objective truth.

I remember a husband and wife in a bitter argument over something he had written in a letter seven years before. She said he had written such and such. He said she was a liar, he had written so and so and on it went.

Both were absolutely certain of the accuracy of their memory, but I discovered that the letter had been burned for at least five years. Only God knows the true facts as to what was in it. The case may seem exaggerated but it is not untypical. The memory can be very selective as to what it stores and what it rejects.

Furthermore, the strain of problem-solving very often puts more pressure on an already stressed relationship than it is able to bear. In marriage counselling I can remember times when I have insisted on getting to the bottom of at least one problem and have succeeded in establishing the objective facts only to find the parties more wounded and bitter towards each other than before we began.

The party proved to be in the right is now justified in his bitterness and even more inflamed by the injustice he has suffered. The party shown to be in the wrong is furious at being stripped of his self-justifying attitude, and more determined than ever to get even somehow. What is more the balance of probabilities in that one case does not reflect the probabilities in all the other problems not yet investigated.

When, however, I look at the way that God reconciles, I discover that problem solving is exactly what God does not do. He does not say, "You have this great problem in your life. Deal with that first before we can even consider reconciliation." He does nothing like that at all.

In fact, when I come to God I do not know what my real problems are. There may be one or two representative sins that I remember, but that is all they really are, representative illustrations of the fact that I am alienated and need to be reconciled. Awareness of my real problems comes only later, much later.

Persons are reconciled, not problems

How then does God reconcile us? It is vital to understand this. It is the divine "How to", and in reconciliation we will never do it better than God does.

Firstly, I note that God finds me as a person. That is his method from the very beginning. When God comes looking for Adam in Eden his cry is first of all not, "What have you done?" but, "Where are you?"

And that was the beginning, not the end of God's search for alienated man. From the Father's bosom Jesus came looking for us. *"The Son of Man came to seek and to save what was lost."*[1]

It dawns on me that you cannot reconcile problems, you can only reconcile people. You solve problems, you reconcile people.

We lose each other in the morass of problems we generate. We cease to relate person to person, and instead we begin to behave towards the other person's behaviour and the other person begins to behave towards our behaviour. Separated from each other we cease to understand, cannot trust, don't care.

Contention, misunderstanding and a host of selfish sinful attitudes cut us off from each other.

It begins almost imperceptibly, thus the confusion in so many broken marriages: "We started out so well. We really loved each other. How on earth did we get ourselves into this mess?"

Reconciliation God's way means that we must first of all find each other as persons, again – or perhaps for the first time.

But we will never find each other through the maze of accumulated problems. All we will find are problems. Therefore we have deliberately to put all our disagreements and differences on one side, put the lot in a "Pending" basket, ignore them until we have found each other. That is how we came to God in the first place.

> "Nothing in my hand I bring
> Simply to thy Cross I cling
> Naked come to thee for dress
> Helpless look to thee for grace ... "

Salvation thus becomes the model for all forms of inter-personal reconciliation. We have to put on one side our agendas, our problems, our rights, our defences, our positions, our perceptions, our interpretations and our presuppositions. Even the principles we think we are standing for and the truth we are defending have to be temporarily set aside. First be reconciled.

You probably ask, "But what about the problems? We can't ignore them and hope they go away. How can we be reconciled except on the basis of justice and truth?"

In his relationship with us, God is certainly very interested in problem solving. Continually he says to me, "You have this problem and I cannot put up with it any longer," or "This is hindering our relationship and you have to face it – right now!"

Here is the important point. God is persistent, patient and quite relentless in problem solving, but *he does it only after we are reconciled, not before.* Problem solving is one of the results of reconciliation, not the means of reconciliation.

Moreover, God deals with our problems only after we are securely held in his unchanging love and we know that our relationship with him does not depend at all on our success in solving the problems. I can face up to major surgery on my life because I know that my acceptance by God and my relationship with him does not depend on my performance in problem solving, it depends on his grace, and that is unconditional.

Just as salvation turns out to be the resource and the model for reconciliation, so sanctification becomes the model for problem solving in relationships. We will explore the implications of this in a later chapter.

Only grace works

The second important point I realised is that God reconciles us on the basis of grace. Years ago, two people in my church got bitterly at odds with each other. Eventually they went to Jesus' instructions in Matthew 18:16–17 because they were aware of the need to settle their disharmony. They followed the Scriptures to the letter: go to the other person alone; if he will not listen, take two or three witnesses; if he will still not listen, tell it to the church.

The results were a shambles. It seemed to me that it would have been far better to have left it as it was in the first place.

I remember driving to some meetings a couple of weeks later and worrying over this. I said, "Lord, they faithfully followed your instructions and it didn't work. What on earth went wrong?"

It was one of those times when I know God spoke to me. He said, very clearly, "You don't understand: it only works on the basis of grace."

Of course! If I say, "I've come half way, now you have to come half way," that is not grace, it is law. If I say, "I've done my share, how about you doing your share?" that is not grace, it is "works".

Grace in human terms is simply doing good to one another with no strings attached. If I say, "I've come to be reconciled to you and there are no strings or conditions attached to that offer," that is grace. If you say to me, "I've come to be reconciled to you and there are no strings attached to my offer", that is grace. On that basis God's plan for reconciliation works perfectly.

That is why the key figures in any reconciliation between deeply divided sections of our society have to be the Christians on both sides of the divide. Only they understand grace because they have been its beneficiaries. Therefore only they can explain it and model it to a hurting world. That is what makes division and strife between Christians and between churches such an unbearable scandal, because we are supposed to be ministers of reconciliation.

Reconciliation and relationship

Finally God reconciles us by receiving us into a relationship. Reconciliation is consummated in communion. You cannot have reconciliation that settles a difference but leaves the parties still at arm's length. Thus it is both a crisis and a process, a crisis point in its beginning and a process in its expression.

Two of the words commonly found in the Bible in the context of reconciliation are important in understanding this. One is covenant, and the other is friendship. Covenant is a bond of personal commitment and loyalty between two parties which is by its very nature everlasting. A time-based covenant is a contradiction in terms. In this it differs from a contract. A contract is a relationship created by the conditions of the contract; if the conditions are changed, the relationship changes. A covenant has obligations and conditions but they are created by the relationship not the other way round. Therefore our reconciliation with God is founded on the new covenant. In the Old Testament the reconciliation between Jacob and Laban was likewise sealed by a covenant.

Marriage is a covenant, and some of the miracles I have seen have been the restoration through reconciliation of broken marriage covenants.

Friendship is like covenant. When Jesus chose to call us his friends he accepted the moral obligation of friendship, that nothing, not even death must ever be allowed to separate friends. *"Greater love has no one than this"* he said, *"that he lay down his life for his friends."* [2]

Jesus laid down his life for us, his enemies, and transformed us into his friends. He sends his Holy Spirit into our hearts that nothing in heaven or earth or all creation will ever separate us from our Friend.

Reconciliation brings us into biblical covenant and friendship with one another, with the moral obligation that henceforth nothing, no difference, no quarrel, no crisis, no question, no dispute will ever be allowed to separate us from each other.

Steps towards reconciliation

How then are we to find one another again and allow God to effect reconciliation between us? If the Cross offers such hopeful grounds, how do we begin to implement it?

The first thing to realise is that we are to take the initiative. Always it is us who have to take the first move, I cannot say, "It is up to him, or her, or them. I didn't start it, they are the ones who created this division." Jesus makes abundantly clear where the moves for reconciliation are to begin. In Matthew 5:23 he says, *"If you are offering your gift at the altar and there remember that your brother has something against you, leave your gift there in front of the altar. First go and be reconciled to you brother; then come and offer your gift."* Reconciliation takes both priority and urgency but note it does not say that I have something against my brother, only that he has something against me. John says, *"Anyone who claims to be in the light but hates his brother is still in the darkness. Whoever loves his brother lives in the light."*[3] If my brother hates me, he is in the darkness and cannot find me, but if I do not hate him, I am in the light therefore I can go and find him.

On the other hand in Matthew 18:15–17 Jesus says that if my brother sins against me, I am still the one who has to take the initiative to show him his fault and try to win him. He may be bound and burdened with guilt, and because I do not have guilt to struggle against I can act more freely and more graciously than he can to achieve reconciliation.

Of course there may very well be a deposit of negative feelings that have to be managed. Some of them, such as resentment or bitterness have to be dealt with unilaterally. Regardless of the attitude of the other person we have to deal with them ourselves because they stand in the way of further progress towards reconciliation. What happens when a relationship goes wrong is that we get wounded and hurt. Bitterness can easily enter and infect the wounds. But if we hold on to the bitterness we effectively lock Christ out of the situation. He cannot come in and heal our hurts if by so doing would be seen to justify our bitter feelings. Letting go of bitterness will not heal us; only Christ can heal us, but when we deal with it, we remove a major hindrance to healing.

To let resentment go is an act of the will. We recognise this in the very expression we use. We say, "I'm holding something against him." If I'm holding it, I can also let it go.

Moreoever, holding on to resentment and bitterness keeps us under the power of the other person. I am not free to choose how to act or feel or behave towards that person because the sight of her, or even the memory, triggers off the resentment and the resentment determines it for me. Let the resentment go, and I am free to choose how I ought and will think or act towards them.

Dealing with these issues is very important for another reaon. It helps us through the difficult task of separating the person from what he or she has done. It is not going through the catalogue of offences and trying to forgive them one by one. That, at this stage is impossible. Rather it is seeing the person as a person, identifying our feelings against that person and choosing to let them go free of what we have been holding in our hearts of vengeance or malice or resentment.

> "I saw something move in the mountains, and I thought it was an animal.
> It came nearer and I saw that it was a man.
> It came nearer still, and I found it was my brother."

Along with this, there is the need for genuine repentance. To begin with we have to realise that both by our actions and our reactions we have sinned against, and grieved the Holy Spirit. He himself is the bond of our union in all relationships in the body of Christ. If I have behaved wrongly towards my wife or my children or my brother or sister in Christ, I grieve the Spirit. If they react wrongly the Holy Spirit is grieved again.

Similarly in our behaviour in the relationship we have also been the offender at least part of the time. We may have broken promises or there may be vows we have made to one another in marriage that we realise we have actually broken or failed to keep. Thereby we rank with the covenant breakers and we need to repent and seek God's forgiveness for these sins.

Then we need to find each other again, as persons. If we have worked honestly through the previous stages, this aspect is often astonishingly simple and easy to do. When our hearts are looking for each other they can find each other like homing pigeons. The process is nowhere captured more vividly and brilliantly than in Jesus' story of the return of the prodigal son.

"But while he was still a long way off, his father saw him and was filled with compassion for him; he ran to his son, threw his arms around him and kissed him." [4]

For those who have a need to grasp the "how to", let us try to take it step by step.

Firstly we need to deliberately put aside our problems, our agendas, our expectations and our future requirements. In other words, all the "But's" and the "Provided that's" have to be resolutely put on hold. The person's behaviour is not what we are dealing with at present, it is the person as person.

Secondly we need to reach out in our heart towards each other. Often there needs to be the reaching out in words and in physical touch. I note how often it speaks of Jesus doing that, moved with compassion, touching, putting his hands on them, taking them by the hand. There was the way he spoke to them – "Son, daughter, little girl, woman."

Sometimes I have seen the surprise in people's eyes, and in their voices at what they have found. They discover that in all their past they have never ever touched the real person before. In groups where there has been bitter discord and division over questions of policy or principle you hear the same thing. "I never knew they were like that," "Take them one by one, they are real neat folk."

Thirdly, coming to each other in that attitude of repentance and humility we can ask for and give forgiveness for our estrangement, and by faith in the reconciling work of the Cross we can receive each other into a new relationship. Note carefully that this is a faith step. It is as much a faith step as receiving Christ for salvation, because it is salvation we are receiving, the work of the Cross to salvage a broken relationship. We are experiencing another level of righteousness by faith, being restored to a right relationship with our fellow. In case this seems strange to you, we find a passage in Job 33:26 when it says God restored a man to his righteous state and from the context you will see that what it means is that God healed him, and restored his body to a right relationship with its environment.

It is here that heart change takes place, and love begins to flow towards those who have become our opponents or our adversaries or our enemies. Trust is reborn in spite of past failures and past disappointments and it becomes possible for us who have broken promises and undertakings and vows in the past to become trustworthy. It is no accident that it was the Cross that made faithful apostles out of Peter who denied Christ and the others who abandoned him in spite of their assertions of loyalty.

It is here also that we look at each other with new eyes, and discover a new sense of value in each other that had long since disappeared, I remember a woman saying at such a point, "I realised our marriage was worth saving after all because he was worth saving, and somehow, I felt worth saving too."

And finally at that point where person meets person there is likely to be evoked that strange, insatiable curiosity to know, and to want to be known.

What happens at this point is very individual and very varied. As far as I can observe it is as individual as people's experience of the new birth because what we are dealing with is not a technique but a personal encounter. For some it is an almost instantaneous transformation, like a sudden conversion. I remember one deeply estranged and wounded couple, coming together after over two years apart, the husband becoming a Christian, their marriage being reconciled and them falling in love all over again and all inside a week. In other cases it is more gradual, the reaching out is, to begin with, more tentative and cautious and there is a real but scarcely perceptible realisation that things are different this time, and that something new and radical has happened between them.

This latter outcome is, of necessity, the more common where a group is involved because individuals in the group come in different ways and at different paces to the point of reconciliation.

But the outworking is always essentially the same – the divide is spanned and those who have been alienated from each other and have lost living contact, have found each other again.

In receiving each other however, we also recognise and admit the need for change. We can now commit ourselves to face the necessary changes that reconciliation will undoubtedly bring and to help each other to change, no matter how uncomfortable and difficult it may initially seem. What we are experiencing at this point is a work of divine grace that gives a new beginning. There is a new dynamic at work. The relationship that emerges is founded on covenant, therefore change, even radical change is in the wind. We cannot slip back into the old ways; they didn't work before, they will not work now. We have a new blueprint. Our commitment is now to build a relationship squarely on the four pillars we discussed in the earlier part of this book – love, trust, respect and understanding.

"I wish," said a middle aged man to me, "I'd heard this twenty years ago when we were first married. I needed a framework and I failed as much because of ignorance as ill will."

Even the problems can be faced with new hope because now we have a secure place to stand on while we tackle them. To the question of problems we can now turn, not before this, but now.

References

1. Luke 19:10.
2. John 15:13; Romans 8:38–39.
3. 1 John 2:9.
4. Luke 15:20.

Chapter 11

Problem Solving in Relationships

We have seen that we are reconciled to God, not on the basis of problem solving but on the basis of grace. But God is very concerned about the problems in our life and in the course of our on-going relationship he gets to grips with specific issues in a persistent and thorough going way. We call this process sanctification. If however, we examine the way in which God does this, we will discover that just as salvation is the model or paradigm for reconciliation, sanctification turns out to be the model for problem solving. By that I do not mean that sanctification of itself settles all relationship problems but that God's method or "how to" in sanctification is the method or "how to" for relational problem solving.

We can summarise the principles that God uses as follows.

Firstly it begins with our secure acceptance by God on the basis of the Cross. Our acceptance and our security do not depend at all on our success in solving problems. We can face up to major adjustments in our character and our lifestyle in the course of God's dealings with us because we know that regardless of our success or failure in meeting such challenges we are always held securely in the unconditional love of the Father. That principle also turns out to be the first essential for successful problem solving in relationships. I now realise that in the early years of my first marriage I was able to face up to what were for me, major adjustments, because I somehow knew that Jenny was unconditionally committed to me and to our marriage and would go on loving me in spite of my problems and my weaknesses. Without an undergirding like this in a relationship we are always in danger of feeling pressured to change, even when the change is desirable, or, what is sometimes worse, feeling that we are entitled to something extra as a bonus because we have managed to change.

Secondly, when we are secure in the knowledge of God's acceptance, the Holy Spirit leads us into progressive, specific repentance for sinful acts and attitudes and the establishment of new patterns of behaviour. It is then that we discover that while we cannot damage or impair or alter God's love for us, neither can we outlast his persistence or con him into overlooking things in us that he knows need to change. We run up against his obdurate loving faithfulness.

In a relationship that is alive and growing there is the same progressive dealing with stumbling blocks and wrong acts and attitudes. One of the things we discover is that somehow it becomes the relationship that demands of us both that we change rather than that either party demand that the other changes his or her ways, "It is not that Lyn has laid anything on me about this," George said to me, "it is just that our marriage requires that I improve my performance in this particular area."

Finally, as we face up to progressive changes in our character and lifestyle so that they come more and more to harmonise with the character of God, we experience more and more joy in our relationship with him. Further, we experience more and more fulfilment as we learn to live for his glory and not our own. The same principle lies at the heart of all human relationships. As we learn to adjust to each other and to harmonise our acts and attitudes with each other's, we will discover increasing joy and delight as we live for each other's fulfilment and not our own. If the ungiven self is the unfulfilled self, then we will also find that the given self is the fulfilled self.

One of the first results of true reconciliation is often that many problems disappear of their own accord. These are the ones that were not really the cause of disharmony so much as the results of it. Similarly attitudes often change so much in the process of reconciliation that major sources of difficulties and discords just cease to exist. When feelings of superiority or inferiority disappear, or aggressiveness or defensiveness are no longer necessary, the conflicts that they cause will also vanish. After a while it becomes possible for us to laugh at ourselves again, and to laugh with each other.

Forbearance

Very often when people are making a new beginning in a relationship they determine never again to allow unresolved problems to pile up; as soon as they strike a problem they will stay with it until it is resolved. The motive is excellent but in reality if they stick with this resolve they are unlikely to get further than afternoon tea time on the second day. The fact is that a whole host of differences and difficulties in relationships do not call for problem solving at all. What they need is what the New Testament calls forbearance.

What such things consist of are our little personal habits or idiosyncracies, our quirks of behaviour, the ways we have of doing things or expressing ourselves that rub the other person up the wrong way. Generally they are things that only become problems because we have already begun to drift apart, distance has already come between us. For example, missionaries have come home from the field in defeat, not because of the climate or health or persecution but because they couldn't stand a colleague who snored or who insisted on sleeping with the window open (or shut).

Forbearance is the ability not to be unduly upset or irritated by the faults or weaknesses of others. It is not just indulgence or mere tolerance or putting up with things. It is an active bearing with and bearing each other's burdens. *"Be patient, bearing with one another in love."*[1] Acceptance has to do with the person, forbearance has to do with his or her behaviour.

It is a priestly virtue according to the writer to the Hebrews. The priest *"is able to deal gently with those who are ignorant and going astray since he himself is subject to weakness."*[2] This points up the two main reasons why we often find forbearance difficult, one a lack of compassion and inability to identify with the other person's failings and two, an unwillingness to face up to our own weaknesses and unexplored tendencies that are probably equally irritating to the other person.

But if we are short of forbearance we can go for it to our great High Priest, *"Consider him who endured such opposition from sinful men so that you will not grow weary or lose heart."*[3]

Forbearance does not mean that the matter is necessarily ignored but it gives the patience and the gentleness to wait for the appropriate time and to approach the matter in a positive and helpful way. When God raises an issue in my life I often marvel that he has put up with it for so long, waiting for the right time to deal with it. Forbearance frees us, in other words, from the need for immediate reaction or the pre-emptive strike.

Furthermore, it gives us the grace to take steps to protect each other from temptation or pressures that we know cause particular problems.

Unresolved hurts from the past

There are other problems that can arise between us that have little in fact to do with the present relationship at all. They are caused by things that have happened to us in the past or outside the present relationship and which have left hurts or wounds that have never been healed or resolved. For example, years ago a parent or a schoolteacher may have devastated our young life with a burst of sarcasm that was almost crippling because it articulated some of the very things we already dreaded might be true about ourselves. For years the memory of that hurt or fear has been buried until it is completely forgotten. But a casual, half joking remark by a friend or colleague happens to use some of those very same emotionally loaded words and a sharp, defensive or bitter retort leaps to our lips. We know it is unfair even as we express it, but we cannot hold it back.

These situations are impossible for the other person to handle because they can see no logical or understandable connection between what they said or did and our reaction. It may very well be that we cannot see the connection ourself and would be hard put to explain the reason for the overkill in our response.

The situation may be even more critical if a person has suffered from a marriage breakdown and has remarried on the rebound or before there has been time for the trauma of the previous relationship to be healed or the attitudinal difficulties that contributed to that breakdown to be dealt with.

It is not enough however to realise that our reactions are not the fault of the other person's behaviour although we need to acknowledge this and put the immediate circumstances right. There is a positive side to it: something that was buried has now surfaced and there is the chance for us to deal with the issue.

Wounds in our feelings can only be healed when we are feeling them, only then are we in touch with the damaged area and can bring it to Christ for him to cleanse and heal. Such experiences are part of our inward journey towards wholeness and we will later be eternally grateful for the innocent remark of a friend or spouse that was the means God used to draw our attention to a festering sore buried inside us.

Unintentional wrongs

Then there is the area of unintentional wrongs. They are at once the easiest and the hardest to deal with. The aspect of intention is central to any concept of moral wrong. I am standing in a bus and it stops suddenly throwing everybody off balance. If somebody steps heavily on my foot, I may be hurt but I am not entitled to get angry at the person because it was accidental, there was no intention to hurt me. On the other hand if I get into a heated argument with somebody and they take a wild swing at me and miss, I am liable to get angry because although they didn't actually hurt me they intended to.

We can, of course, tell untruths about our intentions. We can say, "Sorry, I didn't mean to hurt you" when all the time we know we had that aim in view. Nevertheless there are times when we get hurt by something that is said or done and there was no ill intention present at all. I have a problem here. It seems to me that when repentance is expected, or even where forgiveness is gratuitously given for a consequence that was not intended or foreseen, it runs the grave risk of confusing the issue. The other person may be left with a real sense of injustice because forgiveness presupposes guilt and there was no blameworthy intent at all.

On the other hand, consequences cannot go uncorrected just because they were never meant to produce the effect they did. We cannot pass the results off as merely "unfortunate". Carelessness or thoughtlessness may indeed be blameworthy. We have to put things right as expeditiously, as generously and as equitably as possible. I am responsible for the results of my behaviour even if it produces consequences I did not foresee and did not intend.

Finally there are real wrongs that have to be faced up to and dealt with before we can go on. These cannot be avoided and should not be postponed. If they are not addressed they will bring real strain and tension into the relationship. Moreover if the failure persists we are sowing the seeds of relational breakdown. But how are we to go about dealing with them?

Rehabilitating anger

There is, I believe, an important area of misunderstanding or lack of understanding of the nature and proper place of anger. Conrad Baars, a Christian psychiatrist wrote about the apathy amongst so many Christians towards social evils such as abortion or pornography or poverty or discrimination. He suggested that one of the reasons is that the church's teaching regarding anger has been almost totally negative. Christians cannot love such practices but they have also been taught that it is wrong to be angry. The result is either apathetic defeatism or passionless protest. This mood was caught prefectly in W.B. Yeates" poem *The Second Coming*.

> "Things fall apart, the centre cannot hold,
> Mere anarchy is loosed upon the world;
> The blood dimmed tide is loosed, and everywhere
> The ceremony of innocence is drowned;
> The best lack all conviction, while the worst
> Are full of passionate intensity."

Sadly there is often more passion and intensity of feeling on the side of evil than there is on the side of goodness.

What is anger?
One of the problems is that our language has no ready way of distinguishing between anger as a feeling and anger as behaviour, but the distinction is of crucial importance.

Anger is one of our God-given emotions, it is in fact one of the emergency arousal emotions and its function is to release internal energy to enable us to face a crisis or danger. Some of the other words we associate with anger express this aspect of energy; think, for example, what is conveyed by such terms as indignation, zeal, fury or wrath.

Anger as a feeling is however, in itself morally neutral. It can lead either to sinful behaviour or to righteous behaviour.

142

"In your anger, do not sin. Do not let the sun go down while you are still angry and do not give the devil a foothold."[4] This distinction between feeling and behaviour is clearly seen in the relationship between Cain and Abel. We read in Genesis 4:6–7 *"So Cain was very angry and his face was downcast."* Then God speaks to Cain, *"Why are you so angry? Why is your face downcast?"* Note the feelings are only questioned, they are not condemned, but then comes the warning, *"If you do right, will you not be accepted? But if you do not do right, sin is crouching at your door, it desires to have you, but you must master it."* The crucial point with Cain, as it is with us, was his behaviour, not his feelings.

When is anger necessary?

Anger is thus an emotional reaction whose purpose is to arouse us to take the kind of action that ought to be taken in situations like the following:

1. To correct an offence or a wrong done to us or to those we love or to those for whom we have a moral responsibility. If we do not get angry at the evidence of cruelty to children or women or the helpless or animals there is something gravely wrong with our moral sensibilities.
2. To defend ourselves, or those we love or things we hold dear against harm or danger, and against the repetition or continuance of a harmful act.
3. To demand an apology or repentance or restitution or retribution for an offence or wrong that has been committed, and
4. To let the other person know how we feel so that he or she is given the opportunity to put things right and to treat us more justly or more charitably in the future. Can you recall a time when you at last got really angry at a person's wrong behaviour and they said in startled surprise, "I'm sorry, I had no idea you felt like that about it."?

You do not have to read far in the Gospels to realise that there were times when Jesus got angry. When he drove the money changers from the temple, it takes no great effort to imagine the tone of his voice, *"How dare you turn my Father's house into a market!"* The verse of scripture that came to mind to the disciples, awed by his indignation was, *"Zeal for your house will consume me."*[5]

The picture is of controlled power and channelled moral zeal. It is summed up in the most vivid of all phrases used to describe the divine energy let loose against sin and evil, *"The wrath of the Lamb."*

When is anger justified?

We have already referred to the way in which feelings and behaviour run together but they are separable and must be kept distinct. The question that has to be faced is, "How do I know whether my anger is justified in the first place?"

Emotional reactions are largely the result of our perception, so that if I perceive a danger that is not actually there at all, or a threat that is non-existent, I will respond in unnecessary and useless anger. Similarly, if what is being protected is not something I should be defending in the first place, my anger will again be unjustified. For example, I may be defending my pride or conceit about myself or some quite false and worthless opinion. What needs to be corrected in such cases is my perception and my discernment, I need to "see" things in their proper perspective.

It is important to understand that the emotions although they are powerful motivators of behaviour, are not meant to be the guides to our behaviour. Our behaviour is meant to be directed by our conscience, by our reason and by our will. Anger may arouse me to meet what I perceive as a danger but I am not to be carried away by that anger. I am to decide on the correct response according to my understanding and my spirit. The emotions are in fact so built that they will accept a decision by those higher faculties, and the energy they provide is still available to empower the response.

Even if the right response is to do nothing, for example to forbear or to forgive, the emotions are not repressed or denied by that decision. In fact by accepting that decision of the will the emotions are still fulfilled and not frustrated.

Another word used to describe the emotion of anger is temper. The original meaning of the word is very interesting, we use it to describe the process of hardening steel. Anger is meant to harden us to face the crisis the way steel is hardened when it is tempered. But if the emotional energy of anger is allowed to run wild, we say, "I lost my temper" which is actually what happens. We lose the ability to handle ourselves in the fray, like a boxer who goes berserk.

The distinction between feelings and behaviour can also help us to see how anger can be channelled into creative reconciliation. Firstly we need to recognise and confront the anger in ourselves, to decide whether it is legitimate, whether it is justified, or whether, in fact, there is an issue that needs to be faced.

If so, we need to recognise and accept the anger and allow its arousal energy to provide the drive to enable us to face up to the situation. If there is an offence or wrong that has to be dealt with then we need to do so with honesty and compassion. Anger and compassion are not incompatible. The issues need to be squarely faced before the matter of forgiveness can be dealt with. In fact premature forgiveness or an attempt to shortcircuit the unpleasantness too often merely results in the whole thing being buried. The same thing happens when people are so afraid of anger that they repress it before it has a chance to express itself. In both cases the anger goes underground to breed resentment. Resentment means to feel over and over. It can also produce malice, bitterness and depression. Remember Blake's poem, *The Poison Tree*:

> I was angry with my friend
> I told my wrath, my wrath did end
> I was angry with my foe
> I told it not, my wrath did grow
>
> And it grew both day and night
> Till it bore an apple bright
> And my foe beheld it shine
> And he knew that it was mine
>
> And into my garden stole
> When the night had veiled the pole
> In the morning glad I see
> My foe outstretched beneath the tree

The way to forgiveness

When an issue has been faced, the wrong has to be acknowledged, responsibility accepted and forgiveness sought. Nothing as qualified and diluted as an apology will do. "I apologise" is often far short of the necessary admission of wrong. I can apologise and privately feel you deserved all you got – but you now have no come back because I have apologised.

I need to acknowledge frankly and humbly, "I was in the wrong. I am responsible for offending you. I ask you to forgive me."

Sometimes we may need to make or offer restitution, restoring to the injured party in some acceptable way, what he or she has lost, or its equivalent. Restitution is a good indicator of repentance but again its specific form can best be decided between parties who are already reconciled to each other.

When the person who has been in the wrong acknowledges the wrongdoing and asks forgiveness, it must always be given, even, Jesus said, to seventy times seven.[6] But let us clear up some misunderstandings that often confuse the whole business of forgiveness.

Firstly, forgiveness is not saying that something that was wrong is right, nor is it saying that it doesn't matter. I remember a woman trying to forgive her husband's break up of their marriage when he brought his new girlfriend into the home and expected his wife to housekeep for them. She said, "How can I forgive it when it was so wrong?" Forgiveness in this sense is different from pardon, only God can pardon our sin. Forgiveness is dealing with our feelings and our response towards the one who has injured us. It is letting them go free of recrimination or retribution as far as our desires are concerned.

When we have been asked for forgiveness it is the choice of our will to give it. We hold something against them with our will, and with our will we can let it go. And forgiveness effectively finishes the issue because when I forgive the other person, what I am saying to them is this – "I will never mention this to you ever again – it is forgiven. I will never mention it to anyone else again – it is forgiven. I will never mention it ever to myself again in brooding or self-pity – it is forgiven."

With forgiveness like that, angry feelings against each other quickly subside. If they do not do so, Jesus gives the soundest psychological advice, every time the negative feelings emerge, pray for the other person, bless him or her and if you have the chance, do them good. The negative feelings will quickly evaporate.

What if there is no response?

We have repeatedly pointed out the essential mutual element in relationships. They cannot be formed unilaterally, maintained unilaterally or reconciled unilaterally. What happens when the other party refuses to be reconciled or refuses to admit the existence of a problem or any responsibility for it?

The ultimate release for our feelings in painful situations like this is unilateral and unconditional forgiveness. *"Father forgive them for they do not know what they are doing."*[7] This does not achieve reconciliation but it releases us from the power of the situation and prevents the intrusion of malice and resentment. Jesus went back to the Father without a single vengeful or bitter thought against those who stubbornly refused to be reconciled to him and deliberately and cruelly killed him. Once we forgive we can be healed from any legacy of woundedness and hurt. We may need to trust the future of the relationship into God's hands, if indeed it has any future, but our growth and our wholeness and our peace are no longer threatened by it.

References

1. Ephesians 4:2.
2. Hebrews 5:2.
3. Hebrews 12:3.
4. Ephesians 4:26.
5. John 2:16–17.
6. Matthew 18:22.
7. Luke 23:34.

Appendix A

Restoring Broken Trust

The restoration of trust is so difficult and problematic that every breach of trust ought to be treated as reprehensible even in what may seem to be minor matters. It is certainly not taken seriously enough today, as though, if I break my word, an apology or a good excuse is all that is needed to reinstate me as someone who can be trusted.

When trust has been broken, any real process of restoring it must involve the following four steps, none of which can be omitted, fudged or glossed over.

1. Repentance

True repentance involves much more than a mere apology or an expression of regret for what has happened. It requires on the part of the offender:

(a) **A sincere acknowledgement that a righteous law of God has been broken and that it was wrong to break it.** The law that has been broken is the law of truth and faithfulness, and the breach is an offence against the character of God who is the Faithful and True[1] and whose word is trustworthy and true.[2]

(b) **A sincere acknowledgement of personal guilt, without excuse or rationalisation.** Rationalisation is finding a reason for our behaviour that is not the real reason but is one that is more comfortable for our ego to live with.

(c) **A sincere intention to amend and to be obedient in future to the law that has been broken.**

149

(d) **Faith that the offended party is willing to forgive, and does so, not only as one who has suffered personal injury but as one who righteously resents the offence committed against the law of God**. This is extremely important. For the wrongdoing to be adequately dealt with, forgiveness must be taken as seriously as repentance, and must not be dismissed with, "Never mind, it doesn't matter." The one who forgives, must in forgiving still preserve a high regard for the law that has been broken.

2. Restitution

This is of extreme importance, not to forgiveness as such, but to the matter of restoration. The key passage dealing with breach of trust is Leviticus 6:2–6 which stipulates that if a person deceives his neighbour about something entrusted to him, or if he cheats him or swears falsely,

1. He must return what was entrusted to him or whatever he swore falsely about,
2. He must make restitution in full, add a fifth in value to it and return it to the owner,
3. He must bring a guilt offering for the priest to make atonement for him.

Restitution is neither punishment nor earning forgiveness, it is making amends or reparation for the wrong that has been done, so that relationships can be restored. It may involve things like a public apology if the breach of trust has affected a body of people, or it may involve some voluntary service to the person who has been let down, or the giving up of certain freedoms or interests in order to give more time to a wife who has been offended against. The particular form that restitution should take should arise out of mutual agreement between the parties as to what is appropriate and healing in terms of the relationship.

3. Redemption

We have seen that the only place where we can find a resource that is able to restore trust is the Cross of Jesus Christ. The death of Jesus was the ultimate expression of human trust, *"Father into your hands I commit my spirit."*[3] He let the outcome of his very destiny go out of his hands into the hands of the Father. Because of this, there is at the Cross a divine source of trust, that can give a person the confidence to trust again after trust has been lost beyond recovery. At the same time it can make the unfaithful and disloyal person able to be trusted and worthy of trust.

4. Reordering

Another vital aspect of restoration that is too often neglected, is the willingness to spend time rebuilding the areas of our life that have proved to be flawed. This is the work of sanctification that follows the act of faith in redemption. Deliberate discipline is necessary even though it is often a painful process to go through. Often it is helpful to have a mentor, a spiritual friend who can be both compassionate and objective and who can help the person being restored to see through some of the unconscious defence mechanisms that blind them to the truth.

Reordering needs to address the following main issues:

(a) What is the nature of the failure? What happened?

There may be one major and obvious breach of trust that has brought disaster or there may be a tangled skein of dishonesties, evasions, deceits and broken promises that need to be patiently unravelled to establish the facts. Often there is a great deal of confusion in the mind of the offender that makes it impossible for him to see the issues with any degree of clarity.

(b) What is the cause of the failure? Why did it happen?

This requires even greater care and insight because we are probing causation. Is the person afraid to commit himself, and if so, why? Does he get into difficult situations through thoughtlessness or carelessness and then seek the easiest way out? Does the failure show up character flaws that need to be addressed, for example, problems with lust, anger or untruthfulness? Does the person have an inordinate desire to be accepted, or loved, or admired?

The aim is to enable the person to understand the problems that have to be dealt with but also to face them with the confidence that they can be overcome.

(c) How can the cause or causes of failure be corrected?
This means developing specific strategies to enable dangerous or unhelpful patterns of behaviour to be discarded and more consistent and helpful patterns to be learned in their place. Ministry may be needed for emotional or inner healing or to break bondages or ties whose existence has been discovered, but the essential thing is to go beyond understanding the nature of the problem, and to begin to take remedial action.

At the same time that the remedial work is under way, steps also need to be taken to build trustworthiness as described earlier (pages 52–54).

(d) How can we know that the weakness or failure has been overcome?
Time is needed, not only for the person's commitment to the prescribed courses of action to take effect but also for the dealings of God in his or her life. But encouragement is also necessary and recognition of the progress being made until the person functions with growing confidence in the areas where he has previously failed.

Restoration where capacity to trust has been damaged

A person who has trusted but has been let down and often, may eventually be so hurt and damaged that they find it impossible to trust anybody ever again. The Psalmist seems to have had this experience; *"I believed; therefore I said, 'I am greatly afflicted.' And in my dismay I said, 'All men are liars.'"*[4]

For such people, the grace of God that enables them to begin to trust again may need to be accompanied by:

Healing of wounds in the human spirit and the emotions
(a) It is essential for the person to forgive those who have let them down or betrayed their trust, and to let go all resentment and bitterness. If I hold on to bitterness I effectively lock Christ out because he cannot heal me if by so doing he would seem to justify my bitter feelings.

(b) It is important for the person to realise that Jesus knows what it feels like to be the victim of disloyalty and betrayal. But because he suffered to the uttermost in all these ways he is able to heal us to the uttermost.

(c) Healing should be ministered in the power of the Holy Spirit, the one who can take the healing that flows from the Cross and bind up our broken hearts.[5]

An examination of the reasons for the broken trust

It is essential to probe the circumstances surrounding the broken trust as there may be important lessons to be learned from the situation, or there may be moral or spiritual issues that may have to be dealt with, such as:

(a) Was trust placed presumptuously or foolishly, for example, without knowing the character of the person being trusted or ignoring clear warning signals?

(b) Was trust placed for wrong or self-centred reasons, for example, to secure personal advantage or as part of a relationship that itself was wrong?

(c) Was the trust itself idolatrous, that is, was it trusting a person for things that we are meant to trust God for, for example, for unconditional unchanging love and acceptance? If this is so, the fault is not that of the person who failed to give what only God can give.

Active encouragement of the person's trust in God

The person's ability and willingness to trust God needs to be encouraged and reinforced. They need to discover the rock beneath their feet. *"To you O Lord I lift up my soul; in you I trust, O my God ... No-one whose hope is in you will ever be put to shame."*[6] The most bruised and broken heart can take refuge in him.

The participation of someone trustworthy so that the damaged person can safely venture to begin to trust again

The rules for building trust also apply here, but note particularly:

(a) Start small, the first steps need to be simple and safe.

(b) Give the person time to be comfortable with the measure of trust they have been able to give. Let them set the pace.

(c) Build little by little, be patient, don't go too far too fast.

(d) Reinforce every successful step taken, and give encouragement if at any time they fail. Simply start all over again.

(e) Return their trust. The person receiving trust has to be seen as taking the same risks of trusting as they are taking.

References

1. Revelation 9:11.
2. Revelation 22:6.
3. Luke 23:46.
4. Psalm 116:10–11.
5. Isaiah 61:1.
6. Psalm 25:1–3.

Appendix B

The "One-Another" Syndrome

There are a considerable number of passages in Scripture which emphasise the mutuality of relationships. They are distinguished with the phrase *"one another"* or *"each other"* and they form an important resource for relation-building.

They are summarised here under the headings of the four factors that we have discussed in this book.

Love

1. *Love one another* (John 14:34; John 15:12, 17; Romans 13:8; 1 Peter 1:22; 1 John 3:11; 1 John 4:8).
2. *Be devoted to one another* (Romans 12:10).
3. *Have concern for each other* (1 Corinthians 12:25).
4. *Be kind to one another* (Ephesians 4:32; 1 Thessalonians 5:15).
5. *Bear with one another* (Colossians 3:13; Ephesians 4:2).
6. *Forgive one another* (Ephesians 4:32; Colossians 3:13).
7. *Comfort one another* (1 Thessalonians 4:18).
8. *Be hospitable to one another* (1 Peter 4:9).
9. *Serve one another* (Galatians 5:13).
10. *Carry each other's burdens* (Galatians 6:2).
11. *Pray for one another* (James 5:16).
12. *Be compassionate to one another* (Ephesians 4:32).
13. *Greet one another with a kiss* (1 Corinthians 16:20; 1 Peter 5:14).
14. *Do not wrong one another* (Leviticus 25:14).
15. *Do not deprive one another* (1 Corinthians 7:5).

Trust

16. *Submit to one another* (Ephesians 5:21).
17. *Confess your sins to one another* (James 5:16).
18. *Speak the truth to one another* (Zechariah 8:16).
19. *Live in harmony with one another* (Romans 12:16).
20. *Do not lie to one another* (Colossians 3:19).
21. *Do not slander one another* (James 4:11).
22. *Do not grumble against one another* (James 5:9).
23. *Do not go to law against one another* (1 Corinthians 6:6).
24. *Do not provoke and envy one another* (Galatians 5:26).

Respect or honour

25. *Accept one another* (Romans 15:7).
26. *Encourage one another* (1 Thessalonians 5:11; Hebrews 3:13; Hebrews 10:25).
27. *Build one another up* (Romans 14:19; 1 Thessalonians 5:11).
28. *Belong to one another* (Romans 12:5).
29. *Honour one another* (Romans 12:10).
30. *Wash one another's feet* (John 13:14).
31. *Consider one another better than yourself* (Philippians 2:3).
32. *Be humble towards one another* (1 Peter 5:5).
33. *Spur one another on* (Hebrews 10:24).

Understanding or knowledge

34. *Have fellowship with one another* (1 John 1:7).
35. *Be at peace with one another* (Mark 9:50).
36. *Teach one another* (Colossians 3:16; Romans 15:14).
37. *Admonish one another* (Colossians 3:16).
38. *Speak to one another* (Ephesians 5:19).

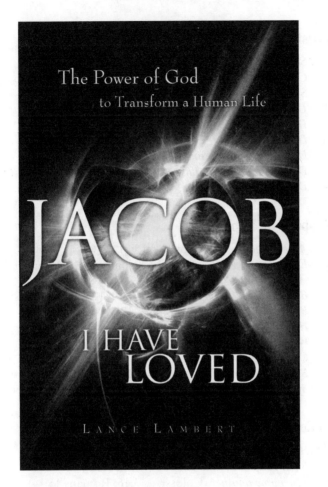

When God deals with us it is often in deeply mystifying ways. There is no greater example of how God shapes a person than through the remarkable story of Jacob. *Jacob I Have Loved* is far more than a mere biblical overview of the story of Jacob. It is an outstanding illustration of God's desire to utterly transform our fallen inner nature. Despite a twisted, deceiving, sinful heart Jacob nonetheless inherited God's richest blessings and became one of the patriarch's of our faith. Jacob's story is an integral part of the history of divine redemption. This book is about the power of God to transform a human life. Jacob's story is our story.

Jacob I Have Loved: The Power of God to Transform a Human Life
By Lance Lambert
£10.99 | 978-185240-4765 | 224pp | Sovereign World Ltd

THE TRUTH & FREEDOM SERIES

GOD'S COVERING

A PLACE OF HEALING

DAVID CROSS

God's covering is an expression which describes the spiritual protection and nurture which God provides for all those who are in a covenant relationship with Him. You cannot see His covering but you can certainly experience the effect which it has. Without Jesus, the world cannot truly understand God's covering but all of mankind desperately needs it! Outside this shelter, men and women are vulnerable to a hostile spiritual realm which governs this world and all those who remain in rebellion to the One who created them.

God's Covering: A Place of Healing *by David Cross*
£7.99 | 978-185240-4857 | 192pp | Sovereign World Ltd

We hope you enjoyed reading this Sovereign World book.
For more details of other Sovereign books and
new releases see our website:

www.sovereignworld.com

If you would like to help us send a copy of this book
and many other titles to needy pastors in developing countries,
please write for further information
or send your gift to:

**Sovereign World Trust
PO Box 777
Tonbridge, Kent TN11 0ZS
United Kingdom**

You can also visit **www.sovereignworldtrust.com**.
The Trust is a registered charity.